85

LETTERS FROM
THE FEDERAL FARMER
TO THE REPUBLICAN

LETTERS

FROM THE

FEDERAL FARMER

TO THE

REPUBLICAN

EDITED BY

WALTER HARTWELL BENNETT

THE UNIVERSITY OF ALABAMA PRESS
University, Alabama

Library of Congress Cataloging in Publication Data

Main entry under title:

Letters from the Federal farmer to the Republican.

   Attributed to R. H. Lee.
   Originally published anonymously in 2 separate
pamphlets, printed by T. Greenleaf, New York (1787 and
1788, respectively), and paged continuously; the 1st
pamphlet with title: Observations leading to a fair
examination of the system of government proposed by the
late convention; and the 2d with title: An additional
number of letters from the Federal farmer to the Republican.
   1. United States. Constitutional Convention, 1787.
I. Bennett, Walter Hartwell, 1907-   II. Lee,
Richard Henry, 1732-1794. III. Observations leading to
a fair examination of the system of government proposed
by the late convention. 1977. IV. An additional
number of letters from the Federal farmer to the Republican. 1977.
JK146.L46   342'.73'024   77-8383
ISBN 0-8173-5113-2

This edition of the
Federal Farmer's Letters is published to
celebrate the two-hundredth anniversary
of the revolutionary political events
that took place in America between 1776 and 1791
and is dedicated to Mae Maxine Purcell Bennett,
who has spent much of her life
teaching college students the principles
of American government and the
historical background of those principles.

PREFACE

The events commemorated by the publication of this book include the American Revolution, which began with the adoption of the Declaration of Independence in 1776; the framing and ratification of the United States Constitution in 1787 and 1788; and the framing and ratification of the ten amendments to the Constitution that became effective in 1791 and comprise the federal Bill of Rights. The letters we know today as the *Letters from the Federal Farmer to the Republican* were occasioned by the framing and ratification of the Constitution; but they are to be known also for the basic political philosophy that is represented by them. That is predominantly the political philosophy of the Revolution and the Bill of Rights.

The first sentence of the first letter in the series alludes to letters as having been addressed by the author to the Republican the preceding winter and having as their subject a well-balanced national government for the United States. But nothing more is said about these earlier letters. If written the preceding winter, they of course antedated the framing of the Constitution.

The letters contained in this edition were first published in two separate pamphlets, both printed in New York City by Thomas Greenleaf, publisher of the *New York Journal*. The first pamphlet, comprising Letters I–V, appeared in the fall of 1787 and is entitled "Observations Leading to a Fair Examination of the System of Government Proposed by the Late Convention; and to Several Essential and Necessary Alterations in It. In a Number of Letters from the Federal Farmer to the Republican." The second pamphlet, comprising Letters VI–XVIII, appeared during the first half of 1788 and is entitled "An Additional Number of Letters from the Federal Farmer to the Republican; Leading to a Fair Examination of the System of Government Proposed by the Late Convention; to Several Essential and Necessary Alterations in It; and Calculated to Illustrate and Support the Principles and Positions Laid Down in the Preceding Letters." The second pamphlet is paged continuously with the first, and the letters of the second pamphlet are numbered continuously with those of the first.

The letters of each of the pamphlets have been reprinted, but until now the entire series has not been reprinted in a single edition. Letters I–V are included in *Pamphlets on the Constitution of the United States,* ed. Paul Leicester Ford (Brooklyn, New York, 1888), and a facsimile reprint of the second pamphlet was published by Quadrangle Books, Chicago, in 1962. Letters I–VII and XVI–XVII are also reprinted in the volume *Empire and Nation,* eds. William E. Leuchtenberg and Bernard Wishy (Englewood Cliffs, New

Jersey: Prentice Hall, 1962), pp. 87–173. The letters in the present edition have been reprinted from the original printed texts, with the addition by the editor of a separate title for each letter and a synoptic table of contents for the entire series. Spelling and printing errors that appeared in the original texts have been corrected.

The editor acknowledges with gratitude financial assistance in the preparation of this edition that was received from The University of Alabama Research Grants Committee. He is indebted to staff members of the University's Gorgas Library for their efficient and unfailingly courteous service. Thomas Griffin Barber, Charles Rayburn Barton, and Marshall Douglas Ghee, student assistants in the Department of Political Science of the University, all helped toward insuring the accuracy of certain of the information contained in the editor's introduction. Finally, special thanks are due to Paula J. Franks, secretary in the Department of Political Science, for her service as typist, which she has rendered with her customary care and cheerfulness, and to staff members of The University of Alabama Press, whose advice on technical matters during the final stages of preparation of the manuscript for publication has been especially helpful.

WALTER H. BENNETT

The University of Alabama
April, 1977

CONTENTS

for opponents and advocates to the Constitution—Tactics employed by the advocates—
Principles and institutions of government which are best suited to America—Principles
and institutions of existing American governments.

EDITOR'S INTRODUCTION

I

On September 20, 1787, the Congress under the Articles of Confederation, then in session in New York City, received from the recently adjourned Federal Constitutional Convention in Philadelphia that body's proposal for a new Constitution of the United States. Eight days later, Congress, in accordance with the recommendation of the Philadelphia Convention, directed by unanimous vote that the document be transmitted to the states to be acted upon by state conventions.[1] The seventh article of the document provided that the ratifications of the conventions of nine states would be sufficient to establish the Constitution between the states ratifying it. But before Congress acted, opposition to the Constitution began. An attempt was made to get Congress to amend the document before it was sent on to the states.[2] After that attempt failed, there began to be efforts to have the state conventions initiate proposals for amendment, and there was also agitation for the calling of a second general convention. The latter body, it was assumed, would consider all proposals for amendment and make desirable changes in the document before it was ratified.

By midsummer, 1788, conventions in eleven states—two more than the number required by the seventh article to put the proposed Constitution into effect—had ratified it in its original form. Nevertheless, the struggle for amendments had not been a fruitless struggle. A number of state conventions, even though giving their assent to the document in the form in which it had come from the Philadelphia Convention, adopted elaborate proposals for amendment to be considered after the new government was inaugurated. Certain of these proposals were to become the basis of the ten amendments comprising the federal Bill of Rights.

The *Letters from the Federal Farmer to the Republican* were written during the ratification controversy and were part of the effort to secure amendments to the Constitution. The five letters comprising the Federal Farmer's first pamphlet bear dates that begin with October 8, 1787, and end with October 13 of that year. Letter IV is dated October 12, 1778, but this date is certainly an error, as the letter relates to the draft Constitution and continues a discussion begun in Letter III. The remaining thirteen letters—i.e., those comprising the second pamphlet—bear dates that begin with December 25, 1787, and end with January 25, 1788. Thomas Greenleaf, the printer of both pamphlets, advertised them for sale in his *New York Journal*. The first pamphlet was advertised by him on November 8, 1787, and the advertisement was repeated in subsequent issues of the *Journal* over a period of several months. A half-column advertisement of the second pamphlet appeared in the *Journal* for the first time on May 2, 1788. This advertisement was repeated in most issues of this newspaper published between that date and the end of July of that year.[3] Both pamphlets were reviewed in *The American Magazine* in May, 1788.

Who the author of the two pamphlets was is uncertain. Within a few weeks after the first pamphlet began to be advertised, Richard Henry Lee of Virginia was addressed as its author in an open and extremely critical letter written by a supporter of the Constitution and appearing in the *Connecticut Courant* over the pseudonym "New England."[4] This open letter was reprinted in other newspapers soon after its original publication, and later Lee came generally to be accepted as author of the Federal Farmer's pamphlets. For approximately a century beginning in the 1870's, he was regularly listed as the author in bibliographic compilations published in the United States and was referred to as author of the pamphlets in numerous works by American scholars dealing with the controversy over the ratification of the Constitution. No positive proof has been presented in print in recent years that he was not the author, but an article by Gordon S. Wood published in the *William and Mary Quarterly* in 1974 makes clear that the question of authorship of the Federal Farmer's pamphlets is not today a settled matter.[5]

Lee was serving in Congress as a delegate from Virginia when that body received the Constitution from the Philadelphia Convention, and he appears clearly to have been the chief instigator of the movement to have Congress amend the document before ordering its transmittal to the states. He drafted specific proposals for amendment and presented them to Congress, only to see them pushed aside when Congress made its decision to send the Constitution to the states in its original form.[6] After this, as his private correspondence shows, Lee hoped that the conventions called in the states to consider the Constitution could be prevailed upon to initiate proposals for amendment, and he repeatedly urged the calling of a general convention which might consider all such proposals and make desirable alterations in the document before it should be finally adopted.[7] In the late spring of 1788, he was still agitating for amendments, although by now he appears to have lost all hope of preventing the adoption of the Constitution until amendments were added, observing that some of the friends of amendments feared the calling of a general convention to consider them lest such a procedure might "risk the whole." He now proposed conditional ratification by Virginia and hoped that the example of this state would influence four other states that were still to take action on the subject of ratification. The ratifying convention to be assembled in Virginia would agree upon proposals for amendment and then ratify the Constitution with the proviso that the state would be disengaged from its act of ratification two years from the assembling of the first Congress under the Constitution, unless by the end of this period the proposals had become a part of the Constitution in accordance with the procedures specified in the document for its amendment.[8] But this plan for conditional ratification failed to gain the support that would have been required for its adoption.

An examination of Lee's known writings reveals sentiments regarding the Constitution that are on many points strikingly similar to views expressed in the Federal Farmer's letters. In both instances, the position is taken that there is much in the Constitution that is good and that through careful revision the document can be made acceptable. In several letters addressed by Lee to individuals in the fall of 1787, he alludes to the desirable features of the Constitution, using such terms as "excellent regulations," "good regulations," and "useful regulations." In a letter to George Mason on October 1, 1787, Lee, after referring to the "great many excellent regulations" contained in the Constitution, goes on to observe that the document could, if "reasonably amended," be a "fine system."[9] In his fifth letter, the Federal Farmer refers to the Constitution as containing "many good things," and he observes in his sixth letter that the Constitution affords a better basis on which to build than the existing American Confederation. In various letters addressed by Lee to individuals during the fall of 1787 and winter and spring of 1788, and in the Federal Farmer's letters, there are complaints that the proposed Constitution does not contain a bill of rights, that the Senate which is to be created will have too much authority over the executive, particularly in the making of executive appointments, and that the House of Representatives will be too small to give adequate representation to the people.

If Lee and the Federal Farmer were not the same person, the two men reflect in much the same degree the liberal and republican idealism of the American Revolution. The European Enlightenment and the English common law tradition—both powerful influences on American thought during the Revolutionary War era[10]—obviously had much to do with shaping the political thought of Lee and the Federal Farmer. In his private correspondence, Lee cites repeatedly the Frenchman Baron Montesquieu, among Enlightenment thinkers, and in commenting on the proposed Constitution, refers to Blackstone, Holt, and Mansfield among English common law jurists.[11] The Federal Farmer quotes from Montesquieu, the Italian Marquis Beccaria, and the Swiss Jean Louis De Lolme. In addition, he cites Coke, Blackstone, Holt, Mansfield, and Hale among English common law jurists.[12]

There is in the Federal Farmer's letters unmistakable evidence of the influence of some of the same basic notions about governmental forms that one encounters in Lee's letters of the Revolutionary War era. In both instances, it is assumed that republicanism demands a full representation of the people. On the other hand, republicanism is seen as quite compatible with a mixed constitution—i.e., a constitution that was understood to achieve a balance between different orders within society, consisting of a royal order, an aristocratic order, and a democratic order, or at least two of these. Traceable to the commonwealth period of seventeenth-century England, and ultimately to the ancient Greeks and Romans, this principle of a mixed constitution was common among Americans during the eighteenth century and was of substantial influence as new constitutions were drafted for the republican regimes that came into existence in the American states following the adoption of the Declaration of Independence. Although America had no basic social orders that could be so easily identified as those of England, it was widely accepted that an aristocratic and a democratic order did in fact exist in America and that a bicameral legislature was an appropriate mechanism for balancing these orders against each other. Each of the two houses of the legislature would be dominated by one of the two orders.[13]

Although Lee had no experience as a pamphleteer before 1787, in view of his strong feelings on the Constitution and his evident disappointment after Congress failed to consider his proposals for amendment, it is not difficult to imagine his writing in six days the five letters comprising the Federal Farmer's first pamphlet. Quick reactions in regard to matters about which he felt deeply were characteristic of him. Nor, in view of the favorable reception given his first pamphlet, is it difficult to imagine his writing the "additional number of letters" that comprise the second pamphlet. Bound with this pamphlet was an advertisement boasting that four editions and several thousand copies of the earlier pamphlet had been printed and sold. At least one reprinting of the earlier pamphlet was ordered before the end of 1787 by an organization calling itself the "American Society of Gentlemen."[14] According to plans stated in his private letters, Lee is supposed to have been on his way from New York to his home in Virginia a few days before the earlier pamphlet began to be advertised, and he was in Virginia during the winter and spring of 1788. The latter circumstance, plus unusually severe weather conditions during the winter season, might account for the fact that more than three months passed between the date given for the last letter of the second pamphlet and the date when this pamphlet was first advertised in the *New York Journal*.[15] We have noted that the last letter of that pamphlet is dated January 25 and that it was not until May 2 that the pamphlet was first advertised in the *Journal*. That the later of these dates was the date of publication of the pamphlet is probable.

But Professor Wood, after a fairly extensive investigation, has concluded that Lee was probably not the author of the Federal Farmer's letters. In arriving at this conclusion, he stresses especially certain contrasts which he sees between these lettters and a letter addressed by Lee to Governor Edmund Randolph of Virginia and also stresses the fact that we have no record dating back to the eighteenth century or even the first three decades of the nineteenth century that positively identifies Lee as the Federal Farmer except for the open letter of "New England" in the *Connecticut Courant*. Dated October 16, 1787, the letter to Governor Randolph is similar in general content to letters written by Lee to certain other political leaders about this time. It mentioned some of Lee's objections to the Constitution, and along with the letter was enclosed a copy of the proposals for constitutional amendment that had been made by Lee to Congress. While addressed to Randolph as a private letter, it eventually was made public, appearing in several newspapers and becoming a target of attack by supporters of the Constitution.[16]

Professor Wood observes that the letter to Randolph is less moderate in tone than the Federal Farmer's letters; that while the problem of consolidation and the threatened destruction of the states "lay at the heart" of the Federal Farmer's objections to the Constitution as set forth in his first pamphlet, Lee's letter to Randolph, though written about the same time, evidences no concern over this problem; that while Lee in his letter to Randolph advocated the calling of a general constitutional convention to consider proposals for amendment, the Federal Farmer never mentions the calling of such a convention, trusting, instead, the judgment of the state ratifying conventions on the practicability of amendments; and, finally, that there are differences between amendments called for by Lee in the letter to Randolph and the accompanying proposals for amendment that Lee had offered in Congress, on the one hand, and the changes called for by the Federal Farmer in his pamphlets, on the other. Lee wanted to delete from the Constitution its provision for a vice-president and wanted to include in the document protection against federal commercial regulations that would be harmful to southern interests, neither of which changes were proposed in the Federal Farmer's pamphlets. On the other hand, the Federal Farmer favored a council of revision with authority to veto legislation which receives no mention in Lee's letter to Randolph. The idea of an advisory council to the president is supported both in Lee's letter to Randolph and in the Federal Farmer's letters, but on this matter there is disagreement as to details; in the former instance, the council would be a "privy council" consisting of eleven persons selected by the president, while in the latter instance, it would be an "executive council" of seven or nine members chosen by a process in which both Congress and the people would have a part.[17]

Undoubtedly the various contrasts mentioned by Professor Wood merit attention. Yet, how much weight should be given them is necessarily a matter of judgment, as he would most probably agree. If, as he states, the Federal Farmer's letters are more moderate in tone than Lee's letter to Randolph, this could be because the former were really addressed to the general public while the latter was addressed to an individual person. Although the letter to Randolph was made public, we have no information that would suggest that it was Lee's original intention to make the letter public.

Unless we start with the assumption that Lee and the Federal Farmer are not the same person, we are likely to be puzzled by the lack of any mention in the letter to Randolph of the problem of consolidation so much stressed in the Federal Farmer's first pamphlet. But our puzzlement may vanish, or at least be substantially lessened, if we bear in mind the role played by Randolph in connection with the Constitution and also make the altogether reasonable assumption that Lee may have been disinclined to stress issues on which he understood Randolph to be in disagreement with him. Randolph's position on the Constitution was equivocal; but as chairman of the Virginia delegation to the Federal Convention of 1787, he had presented to the Convention the Virginia plan of union, a plan that evidenced no great concern for the future of the states. The plan envisioned the creation of a general government that would function independently of the states, and that government's legislature would be authorized to negative state "laws" that in its opinion contravened the articles of union. Moreover, the legislature would be authorized to order military coercion of any state failing in its duty under the articles of union.[18] Randolph was one of the delegates who were present at the close of the Federal Convention and who declined to sign the Constitution. Like Lee, he expressed a strong desire to see the Constitution amended, but his suggestions for amendment evidenced no special fear of consolidation and what it would mean for the future of the states. His views on the Constitution, including his reasons for declining to sign the document, are set forth in a long letter by him to the speaker of the Virginia House of Delegates on October 10, 1787. In this letter, he refers in two separate places to the desirability of "a consolidation of the union, as far as circumstances will permit."[19]

Certainly Lee's failure to mention to Randolph the problem of consolidation and its implication for the future of the states should not be taken to mean that Lee did not share the concern expressed by the Federal Farmer over this matter. In fact, Lee for years opposed amending the Articles of Confederation in such a way as to add substantially to the powers of Congress.[20] By the summer of 1787, he had apparently undergone some change of mind, joining in the common complaint among American leaders of this period that the states were failing in their duties as members of the existing Confederation.[21] But he still showed no enthusiasm for the idea of a strong central government. He was still opposed to giving Congress a general authority to regulate interstate and foreign commerce. He would give Congress authority to levy impost duties for revenue purposes but would place strict limitations on Congress' exercise of this authority. He would place the duty collections under state governmental control or take other special measures to insure that the collectors did not misuse the authority given them.[22]

Regarding the vice-presidency, at least one point should be made. While it is true that the Federal Farmer does not make an explicit proposal that this office be eliminated, as Lee proposed to Congress, he does make clear that he has no particular desire to see the office retained. In his third letter, the Federal Farmer states that "the vice-president is not a very important, if not an unnecessary part of the system." Like Lee, he notes that the vice-president, as provided for by the Constitution, may at one time be a part of the legislative branch of government (i.e., as president of the Senate) and at

another time be the chief executive magistrate, evidently meaning to suggest
that such an arrangement involves too much mingling of the legislative and
executive branches.

The fact that Lee suggested instituting protection against the adoption by
Congress of commercial measures that would be harmful to the South and
that no such suggestion is made in the Federal Farmer's letters does not seem
particularly significant insofar as the question of authorship of the Federal
Farmer's letters is concerned. It is to be remembered in this connection that
the Federal Farmer was addressing his appeal both to northerners and to
southerners. Understandably it was when writing to southerners that Lee
tended to emphasize that there was a need to protect the South against
commercial measures that might be harmful to the region. Thus the matter is
stressed by him in letters to George Mason, Edmund Pendleton, and Edmund Randolph, all southerners.[23] Whereas the relatively elaborate proposals set forth in the postscript to Lee's letter to Randolph calls for protection
against commercial regulations that might be injurous to a "minority of the
community," some of the versions of the proposals for constitutional
amendment made by Lee to Congress make no mention of protection against
commercial regulations, although they do call for a constitutional amendment that would require more than a bare majority of votes in Congress to
pass bills.[24]

In the final analysis, there is not really a great deal that is in conflict
between Lee's known proposals for constitutional change, on the one hand,
and those made by the Federal Farmer, on the other. The clearest case of
conflict has to do with the proposals for an advisory council to the president
mentioned above. Here, as we have noted, there is disagreement regarding
the council's name, total membership, and the method by which the members were to be selected. This disagreement could be due to the fact that the
proposals were several months apart. Lee's proposal for a "privy council" was
among the proposals he offered to Congress in September, 1787. On the
other hand, the Federal Farmer's proposal for an "executive council" was not
made until his thirteenth letter, dated January 14, 1788. That Lee could have
changed his mind by this time on the name, composition, and method of
selection of the council is probable.

But why, in Lee's known writings, there should be suggestions that a
general convention be called to consider proposals for constitutional
amendment when the Federal Farmer makes no reference to this matter is
certainly not easily explained except on the assumption that Lee and the
Federal Farmer are different persons. Nor, except on this assumption, is it
easy to explain why one should find the Federal Farmer supporting the idea
of a council of review of federal legislation when Lee makes no mention of
such a council in his known writings. Finally, one who assumes that Lee and
the Federal Farmer are the same person must necessarily be baffled by the
apparently complete silence of Lee, and, with the exception of the writer

using the pseudonym "New England," the complete silence of Lee's contemporaries, on the subject of the authorship of the Federal Farmer's letters. It seems especially noteworthy that no reference to the Federal Farmer appears in the extant correspondence between Lee and men like Samuel Adams and George Mason, who had worked closely with Lee over a period of years and whose general philosophical stance harmonized with Lee's own. Lee wrote to Adams two weeks after the Federal Farmer had finished writing the letters of his first pamphlet and wrote at least one letter to George Mason sometime after the entire Federal Farmer series had been completed, the letters to Adams and Mason being devoted almost exclusively to the proposed Constitution. But there is no reference to the Federal Farmer in either of the two letters.[25]

The evidence supporting the attribution of authorship of the Federal Farmer's letters to Lee, while strong, hardly seems sufficient to justify continuing this attribution. At the same time, we lack evidence that would point to some other person as author. A thoroughgoing linguistic and comparative analysis of Lee's known writings and the Federal Farmer's letters should be helpful in dealing further with the question of the validity of the attribution to Lee. But, for good reasons, such an analysis has not been attempted here. It would necessarily be a major undertaking in itself, and the person undertaking it could have no assurance that its outcome would enable him to settle finally the question of authorship. If the data yielded by the analysis should be against Lee as author, there would remain the question of what other person may have been the author.

II

It is clear from the Federal Farmer's letters that he thinks of himself as a supporter of both federalism and republicanism. Undoubtedly the adjective "federal" in the pseudonym Federal Farmer is intended to suggest an attachment to the principles of federalism, and there is never a suggestion in the letters that the "Republican" to whom they are addressed is an adversary of the Federal Farmer.

We have already made reference to the broad meaning that republicanism had for the Federal Farmer, and nothing further need be said on this matter, at least at this point. But something should be said here concerning the confusion over the term "federal" during the ratification controversy and the meaning the Federal Farmer tended to give to this term. Advocates of the Constitution under the leadership of Alexander Hamilton adopted for themselves the name "Federalists," with the consequence that opponents of the document came to be known as "Antifederalists," a name by which they have been called to this day. But both names are misnomers in the light of the meaning of the term "federal" most commonly accepted by Americans before the Constitution was framed. Between the American Revolution and the Federal Constitutional Convention of 1787, it was generally assumed by Americans that a federal government conformed to the basic pattern of organization laid down in the Articles of Confederation adopted in 1781. The government was created by means of a compact agreed to by sovereign states, and states as corporate entities were represented in the government's policy-making organ or organs, with equal voting rights. To the federal government were delegated powers to deal with foreign affairs, defense, and other matters deemed to be of common concern to all parts of the union; but most governmental powers were reserved to the state governments. Finally, in the exercise of powers delegated to it, the federal government dealt exclusively, or almost exclusively, with the state governments or the governments of foreign countries. It was the state governments that regularly dealt directly with individual citizens, even in respect to federal measures that might call for some kind of compliance by the citizens. The exact opposite of a federal government was a "national" or "consolidated" government. Such a government was a "supreme" government, i.e., one that recognized no constitutional boundaries between itself and state or provincial governments. Its powers were not drawn from states or provinces as corporate entities but from people comprising a single nation. Moreover, it regularly adopted measures to be applied directly to individual citizens and enforced those measures on the citizens.[26]

These distinctions between a federal government on the one hand, and a national or consolidated government on the other, were repeatedly made by the so-called Antifederalists during the ratification debates as they sought to demonstrate that adoption of the Constitution would represent a departure from federal principles.[27] It is fairly obvious from the Federal Farmer's letters that he was much influenced by certain of these distinctions, although he did not accept as ingredients of a federal government all that this term had implied for Americans before 1787 and actually points out in his sixth letter that some of those opposing the Constitution are not true federalists. He notes that participants in the ratification debates include on both sides individuals who are only "pretended federalists." Some of the advocates of the Constitution were only pretended federalists because they wanted to see the state governments abolished, and some of the opponents of the Constitution were only pretended federalists because they either wanted no federal government at all or wanted one that was "merely advisory" in character. Between these two groups of pretenders were "honest federalists," who wished to "preserve *substantially* the state governments united under an efficient federal head."

In his seventeenth letter, the Federal Farmer makes plain that he does not consider it to be an essential ingredient of federalism that states be represented in "the general councils" on an equal basis. But he indicates here that he accepts the notions that a federal government is established by compact between sovereign states, that the government is created for the management of "general concerns," and that those of its measures which apply to individual citizens are as a rule enforced on the citizens only through the agency of the state governments.

The problem of consolidation to which we have referred as being of primary concern to the Federal Farmer in his first pamphlet, of course, was for him, as well as for other Antifederalists, fundamentally a problem of the future of American federalism. In his first letter, he concedes that the new plan of government appears to have some federal features but suggests that the Federal Constitutional Convention had intended the plan to be a step toward the establishment of a "consolidated government." In his third letter, he even declares it to be his view that the powers delegated by the Constitution to the general government include "all the essential powers of the community" and that the powers to be left to the states will be of no great importance. Although he is aware that the Constitution will not take from the states their power to tax, he argues that the states' ability to raise revenue by taxation will be seriously limited by the concurrent existence in Congress and the states of a power to levy "internal taxes." He sees the tax measures of the general government as interfering with those of the states particularly when the governments on both levels tax the same objects and suggests that the general government might even go so far as to suspend a state tax that is found to hamper the general government in the administration of its own tax measures.

The suggestion that the Federal Constitutional Convention had intended the proposed plan of government to be a step toward the establishment of a consolidated government in the meaning the Federal Farmer tended to give to this term was certainly not supported by positive proof. Nevertheless, it cannot be denied that the adoption of the Constitution was to establish an entirely new legal relationship between the general and state governments, and it is noteworthy that the Federal Farmer sensed to a remarkable degree the significance of that relationship. If the relationship was not to be regarded as a step toward a consolidated government, it at least was to change drastically the character of American federalism, opening the way for a great growth in the authority and responsibility of the general government at some future time. In his fourth letter, the Federal Farmer calls attention to the broad language in which the Constitution is written, observing that many of the powers which the document would delegate to Congress are "undefined, and may be used to good or bad purposes as honest or designing men shall prevail." In the same letter, he calls attention to the "necessary and proper clause" of Article I, Section 8, of the Constitution, which authorizes Congress "to make all laws which shall be necessary and proper" for carrying into execution other powers of Congress, and all other powers vested by the Constitution in the general government, or in any of its departments or offices. Finally, in the same letter he calls attention to the "supremacy clause" of Article VI of the Constitution, under which a valid federal law must take precedence over a state enactment.

III

In the Federal Farmer's judgment, the threat to republicanism was no less real than the threat to federalism. He was influenced by the theory, supported by Baron de Montesquieu and widely accepted among Americans in the latter part of the eighteenth century, that a large republic was impossible to maintain for a long period of time unless it was a federal, or in Montesquieu's terminology, a "confederate" republic. Why a federal or confederate republic should not be under the same handicap as a republic that was not federal or confederate was not explained by Montesquieu, but he lists in his *The Spirit of the Laws* a number of disadvantages which he considers to be characteristic of large nonfederal republics but not necessarily characteristic of small ones: (1) In the former, there are men of large fortunes, and such men are not to be expected to practice the moderation that is conducive to a healthy republicanism. (2) The "trusts" which it is necessary to place in a single subject are too considerable. The subject soon begins to think that he might be "happy and glorious, by oppressing his fellow-citizens" and to think that he might "raise himself to grandeur on the ruins of his country." (3) The "public good" is sacrificed to a thousand private views; it is less obvious than it is in a small republic and not as much in the reach of each citizen. (4) Finally, "abuses" are more serious in a large nonfederal republic than in a small one; they have greater "extent" and at the same time are "better protected."[28]

The disadvantages of a large, nonfederal republic as seen by the Federal Farmer are somewhat different from those listed by Montesquieu, but the result is the same—i.e., that the government of a large country like the United States should be federal if it is intended that the government be maintained as a republican government. Specific disadvantages of "extensive republics" as described by the Federal Farmer include: (1) a necessity to resort to unrepublican methods (in the Federal Farmer's terminology, to "force and fear") to secure obedience to laws in the outer reaches of the republics, (2) the inability to guarantee to citizens living at great distances from the seat of government the same benefits that are enjoyed by citizens living at or near the seat, and (3) a special difficulty of insuring that all of the diverse interests of the people, scatttered throughout the republics' territories, will be given their fair share of representation in the public councils.[29]

This last point is the major theme of the Federal Farmer's letters, receiving some attention in nearly all of them and being the principal subject of discussion in Letters VII through X. Various of the letters include suggestions of devices whose purpose is to insure that representatives will be kept responsible to their constituencies. Among these are frequent elections and a provision vesting in the people a right to recall their representatives. But what claimed the Federal Farmer's main attention was the size of the representative assembly and of the election districts in which representatives were chosen. He was one of those eighteenth-century Americans who believed that the ratio of representatives to constituents should be relatively large and that representatives should be elected in single-member territorial districts.

The Federal Farmer was not satisfied by the fact that the Constitution left for later legislative determination the units into which the people of the United States were to be divided for electing representatives.[30] Nor was he satisfied with provisions included in the Constitution and involving the size of the proposed new House of Representatives. The number of representatives a state was to have was to depend on the size of the state's population, but it was not contemplated by the framers of the Constitution that a census of the people living in the various states would be taken before the Constitution went into effect. For this reason, the framers included in the document itself a provision specifying the number of seats to be allotted to each state at the inception of the House. Assuming that each of the thirteen states would ratify the document and avail itself of the privilege of choosing all the representatives it was allowed to choose, the total membership of the House at its inception would still be only 65 persons.[31] Decennial censuses were to be taken after the Constitution went into effect, and after each such census Congress was to reapportion the House membership and might increase it; but, with the exception that every state was to be permitted at least one representative regardless of how large or how small its population was, no state was to have more than one representative for each 30,000 inhabitants.[32] The Federal Farmer contends that representation under these provisions will be grossly inadequate. He would start with a House membership of at least twice the size of the original membership permitted by the Constitution. In addition, he would have the Constitution not simply permit but require that this membership be increased as there were increases in the country's population. He anticipated that under such an arrangement the time might come when further increases would result in an assembly of such size that its functioning as a deliberative body would be impaired. Nevertheless, until such a time was actually reached, he would put no constitutional limit on the size of the House membership.

The Federal Farmer's theory of representation involved a theory of group behavior that is strikingly similar to the theory of "factions" elaborated by James Madison in the tenth essay of *The Federalist*.[33] Terms which the Federal Farmer uses are "classes," "orders," and "parties"; but, like Madison, he has reference to what are known to twentieth-century political scientists simply as interest groups. Both he and Madison start with the premise that men everywhere are selfish and go on to emphasize that groups of men will ever be ready to promote their self-interests, even when by doing so they must engage in actions that are oppressive to the rest of the community. This point is especially stressed by the Federal Farmer in his seventh letter. Merchants, he says here, will be ready to pass laws favorable to themselves but oppressive to farmers, and farmers will be ready to pass laws favorable to themselves but oppressive to merchants. Men who live by government fees and salaries will endeavor to raise them, and people who by their taxes must ultimately pay the fees and salaries endeavor to lower them. There are the public creditors, who seek to get taxes increased; and there are the people at large, who seek to have their tax burdens lessened.

According to the Federal Farmer, the way to prevent one class from oppressing another is to balance class against class; and this balancing, he believes, can be made possible only through proper representation in the legislature. The implication is that all classes must be represented if fair treatment is to be guaranteed to all classes. "A fair and equal representation" is defined in the Federal Farmer's seventh letter as "that in which the interests, feelings, opinions, and views of the people are collected, in such manner as they would be were the people all assembled." The same definition, with slightly different wording, is also given in the second letter.

Such assertions concerning representation were not uncommon in the latter part of the eighteenth-century, but all such assertions in that century should not be taken at their full face value. John Adams advised in 1776 that one chamber of a state's legislature should be "an exact portrait, in miniature, of the people at large." But in the same statement, he commented that "the most natural substitute for an assembly of the whole [people]" was "a delegation of power from the many to a few of the most wise and virtuous."[34] The British statesman Edmund Burke comments in his *Thoughts on the Cause of the Present Discontents,* published in 1770, that "the virtue, spirit and essence of a house of commons consists of its being the express image of the feelings of the nation."[35] But it is notorious that Burke rejected the idea that members of the British House of Commons should simply reflect at a given time the prevailing interests and views of their constituents. On being elected to the House in 1774, he told the electors of his Bristol constituency that the British Parliament was "not a *congress* of ambassadors from different and hostile interests." It was, he said, "a *deliberative* assembly of one nation, with *one* interest, that of the whole." Representatives should subordinate their own interests to those of their constituents, and they ought always to hear and seriously consider their constituents' opinions on matters of public policy; but ultimately the representatives' decisions on such matters should depend upon their own mature judgment.[36]

Unlike Adams and Burke, the Federal Farmer appears clearly to have thought of the ideal representative assembly as one in which members of the various interest groups within society were corporally present. In his second letter, he writes about the desirability of allowing "professional men, merchants, traders, mechanics, etc. to bring a just proportion of their best informed men respectively into the legislature." In his seventh letter, he states that the people should be permitted to choose representatives "from themselves and genuinely like themselves." Finally, he makes it known in his twelfth letter that he considers it to be much more important that there be a "sameness" of interests between representative and constituents and that the representative live in the constituents' district than that the representative possess brilliant talents. Nowhere does he address himself directly to the question of whether members of a representative body should be guided in the final analysis by the opinions of their constituents or be guided by their own judgment; but his theory of human nature and of the way in which interest groups conduct themselves when they are faced by public policy issues that affect them suggests a frame of reference that is very different from that of Burke. The Federal Farmer's frame of reference leads logically to a view adopted by the English utilitarians approximately thirty years later—i.e., that it is really idle to ask how representatives should arrive at their decisions on matters of public policy since their decisions will inevitably be determined by what the representatives consider to be in their own best interest. What becomes important is that care be taken to insure that there will be as close an identity of interests as possible between representatives and constituents.[37] Such an objective as this would seem to suggest the need for some form of "proportional" or "functional" representation similar to those that have been popular at one time or another in certain parts of the western world since the beginning of the nineteenth century.[38] But the Federal Farmer never indicates that he had in mind any plan of representation other than the traditional territorial district plan, with each district electing a single representative.

Not surprisingly the Federal Farmer concluded that it would never be possible to achieve at the national level in the United States a fair representation of all groups of the American people. He did not consider this by itself to be a justifiable cause for complete rejection of the proposed Constitution, but what he was so insistent upon was that the document be amended in such a way as both to reduce drastically the powers to be delegated by it to Congress and to give some assurance that at least a majority of the members of the House of Representatives would come from the middle and lower classes instead of from the aristocracy. Usually the Federal Farmer evidences a great deal of respect for people categorized by him as belonging to "the natural aristocracy," which he estimated in his seventh letter to consist of four or five thousand persons who were in high civil or military positions, were eminent professional men, or were men of large property holdings. What was especially to be guarded against was an "aristocratic faction," a "junto of unprincipled men" having private gain as their chief objective, although often already known for their wealth. But, according to the Federal Farmer's theory of representation, no person of the aristocratic order, regardless of his particular connections or of his motives, could be a suitable representative for people below his social station.

The chief purpose of the Federal Farmer's argument on the subject of representation is really to demonstrate the effect which the size of the United States House of Representatives and of the districts in which its members were to be chosen must have on chances that the House would be under aristocratic domination, or conversely, under the domination of people below the aristocratic rank. Throughout his discussion of representation he assumes that it is only in small election districts that there can be any real competition between the aristocracy and other classes of the community for House seats. In small election districts, candidates for seats who were from the middle and lower classes could be expected to know and to be known by the people whose votes they sought and whose interests and views they shared. But in large election districts, only members of the aristocracy would have the wide reputations that would be required to attract enough votes to make a majority. Thus, while in small districts, candidates from the middle and lower classes could be expected to win a large percentage of the election contests, in large districts the winning candidates would normally be members of the aristocracy. Thus, if the Constitution's provisions for the House of Representatives were adopted as they stood, the House would be dominated by the aristocracy, and the Constitution, according to the Federal Farmer in his fourth letter, became a proposal for "a transfer of power from the many to the few." He assumed that the many were in control of the relatively large legislative chambers of the state governments, but powers vested in these governments were now proposed to be vested in a new general government of the union.

Certainly there can be no disagreement with the view that the size of election districts will ordinarily have much to do with the outcome of elections when the election contests are between socially prominent persons and relatively unknown persons. Yet, whatever may be the merits of the Federal Farmer's general argument, it remains true that his forecast regarding the future of the House of Representatives has been proven to have been wrong in at least one important respect. He professed to believe that adopting the Constitution as it stood would mean that the House would never be increased beyond its original size. Beginning as a small chamber and dominated from the beginning by an aristocratic elite that would be fearful of letting in members who would challenge that elite's dominant position, the House would veto any effort to increase its membership. But regardless of what may have been the class composition of the House at its inception, the fact is that the House did increase in size after that time. After the census of 1790, Congress adopted a reapportionment measure that increased the size of the House, and all of the decennial censuses between 1790 and 1920, except one, were followed by congressional acts increasing the House size.

The one exception was the census of 1840, after which Congress decreased the membership from 242 to 232. The reapportionment act that followed the census of 1910 left the House at 435 members, and since 1910 there has been no change from this figure, except for what happened in the decade of the 1960's. In the 1960's a temporary addition of three representatives was made to the House membership in order to give representation to the newly created states of Alaska and Hawaii; but, after the census of 1970, the membership was again 435.[39]

While emphasizing that the "aristocracy" would have a special interest in keeping the House small, the Federal Farmer neglected to consider the prospect that there would be strong pressure to increase the House membership as particular states experienced substantial increases in population and as new states were admitted to the union. Reapportionment of existing seats has always remained as one of the alternative ways of accommodating any substantial change in the distribution of population from state to state, but this way, when it has been employed, has necessarily meant taking from some states legislative seats that previously had been allotted to them and which they did not wish to lose. That such reapportionment has come to be a regular practice in the twentieth century can only be explained in terms of the widespread conviction that continued increases in the House membership would reduce seriously the capacity of the House to function as a deliberative body.

IV

Notwithstanding the fact that the Federal Farmer and James Madison held similar views regarding group interest in politics, they arrived at very different conclusions concerning representation. This is one of the main subjects on which the views of the Federal Farmer, on the one hand, and the views of James Madison and Alexander Hamilton, the two principal authors of *The Federalist,* on the other, are so directly in contrast. *The Federalist* contains only one reference to the Federal Farmer by name and this reference does not relate to representation. Nevertheless, it is reasonable to suppose that the Federal Farmer was one of the opponents of the Constitution that Madison and Hamilton had in mind in several essays by them that deal with representation. The first of the Federal Farmer's pamphlets was available in print when *The Federalist* essays on representation were written, and the second of the pamphlets was probably in print when Numbers 55 through 58 of these essays were written, numbers that deal exclusively with issues which involve representation and which are covered in the Federal Farmer's second pamphlet.

Like the Federal Farmer, Hamilton sees no prospect of a national legislative assembly in which each class of citizens would be represented by persons belonging to that class. He assumes in the thirty-fifth essay of *The Federalist* that there are people who propose such an assembly and labels the idea as "altogether visionary," going on to observe that such representation would never be realized in practice as long as people were left free to vote as they pleased. But Hamilton's main point here is that a fair representation of all classes of people does not require that each class be represented by some of its own number. He notes that the learned professions form no distinct interest and professes to see no real conflict of interests between the groups of people who depend on the land, or between merchants, on the one hand, and manufacturers and mechanics, on the other. He characterizes "the landed interest . . . in a political view, and particularly in relation to taxes" as being "perfectly united," noting that large and small landholders have a common interest in keeping taxes on land as low as possible and that common interest is always to be considered "the surest bond of sympathy." At the same time, he argues that commerce is so allied to the manufacturing and mechanic arts as to make it possible for merchants to represent the interests of manufacturers and mechanics. In fact, he takes the position that the interests of manufacturers and mechanics can be more effectively promoted in legislative assemblies by merchants than by manufacturers and mechanics themselves. The latter groups were sensible, said Hamilton, that their "habits in life" had not been such as to give them the "acquired endowments" without which in a deliberative assembly the greatest of natural abilities were useless. Thus, the merchants, who had "greater influence and weight, and superior acquirements," became the "natural representatives" both of themselves and of manufacturers and mechanics.[40]

Madison attacks in *The Federalist,* Numbers 55 and 58, the idea that people can be better represented in relatively large assemblies than in relatively small ones. He concedes that representatives should be sufficient in number "to secure the benefits of free consultation and discussion, and to guard against too easy a combination for improper purposes" but also lays it down as a general proposition that the number of men who will in fact direct the proceedings of legislative assemblies will vary inversely with the size of such bodies. Thus he argues that the people could never err more than by supposing that by multiplying their representatives beyond a certain point they strengthened the barrier against the government of a few. Said Madison: "The countenance of the government may become more democratic, but the soul that animates it will be more oligarchic."[41]

In Number 57 of *The Federalist,* Madison points out that the electors of the proposed House of Representatives are to include the poor as well as the rich, the ignorant as well as the learned, the humble as well as the haughty sons of distinguished names; and he states, furthermore, that the candidates from whom the electors will make their choices are not to have any requirements of wealth, birth, religion, or civil profession. He also lists factors which he contends will afford assurance that the representatives will be faithful to their constituents. These include: (1) the regard which the representatives may be expected to have for the nature of their engagements, (2) the representatives' sense of gratitude towards their constituents, (3) the frequent holding of elections, (4) the pride and vanity that must attach a representative to the form of government that has favored his pretentions and given him a share in its honors and distinctions, and (5) the fact that the representatives and their friends, like other people, will be subject to the laws the representatives make.[42]

It remains true, however, that Madison and the Federal Farmer had different conceptions of the role a representative was to play as well as different ideas as to what persons were best qualified to play that role. Although the Federal Farmer never addressed himself directly to the question of what should guide a representative in arriving at the decisions he must make as a member of a legislative body, he leaves no doubt that he considers a true representative to be one who adheres as strictly as possible to the views of his constituents. Madison, on the other hand, considered it to be a responsibility of representatives to "refine and enlarge the public views," a position that is in general harmony with Edmund Burke's theory of what the role of a representative should be. A representative, according to Madison, should be acquainted with the "local circumstances and lesser interests" of his constituents, but he should not be too much attached to these and "too little fit to comprehend and pursue great and national objects."[43]

It is ironic that the persons who most likely would be able to satisfy the qualifications for representative as viewed by Hamilton and Madison would belong to what the Federal Farmer called the natural aristocracy. Hamilton leaves no doubt that he considers "the man whose situation leads to extensive inquiry and information" to be much better qualified to serve as a representative than "one whose observation does not travel beyond the circle of his own neighbors and acquaintances."[44] Whereas the Federal Farmer wanted such an increase in the size of the proposed House of Representatives as he believed would afford assurance that a substantially larger proportion of the members would consist of men from the middle and lower classes, Madison warned that the larger a representative body was the greater would be the "proportion of members of limited information and weak capacities." One of the advantages of having each representative chosen by a relatively large number of voters, he believed, was that the suffrages of the citizens would be more likely to center in men who possessed "the most attractive merit and the most diffusive and established characters."[45] Like the Federal Farmer, Hamilton and Madison were committed to republicanism, but they were not prepared to see the mass of the people given the great weight in the formation of public policy that he would give them.

V

Most of the other objections to the Constitution that were raised during the ratification debates are to be found in the Federal Farmer's letters. They relate mainly to the United States Senate and its relation to the House of Representatives and the federal executive branch; to provisions of the Constitution's third, or judiciary, article; and to the absence from the Constitution of a bill of rights.

The Senate and its relation to the House of Representatives are the chief subjects of the Federal Farmer's eleventh letter. Here he makes explicit his endorsement of the principle of bicameralism for the United States. But he complains that the Senate and the House of Representatives provided for by the Constitution will, unless the document is changed, be composed of men "of the same grade in society," with "similar interests and views, feelings and connections." Such a legislative system, he insists, must be devoid of any of the "genuine balances and checks" that ought to exist between "the different interests, and efforts of the several classes of men in the community." He hints that it would be desirable to have a national legislature that would achieve a genuine balance between aristocratic and democratic orders in accordance with the ancient principle of a mixed constitution but sees no prospect of establishing such a legislature. Not only does he contend that it would be impossible to secure in a national legislative chamber "a genuine representation of the people," but he also notes that it would be impossible to achieve the separation between "aristocratical and democratical interests" that would be necessary in order to create a "genuine senatorial" or "aristocratic" chamber. Nevertheless, the Federal Farmer suggests that the framers of the Constitution have not done all that can and should be done to insure that the Senate and House of Representatives will be different in their class composition. In an effort to bring checks and balances between these chambers to "the greatest degree of perfection practicable," he would, on the one hand, seek to guarantee that a majority of the representatives would be drawn from "the body of the people" and, on the other hand, make the Senate "respectable as to numbers, the qualifications of the electors and of the elected." Specifically what the latter was supposed to mean is left unexplained, but that the Federal Farmer had in mind qualifications for senators and their electors that would have made the Senate more representative of property interests is probable. In any event, he noted that a "senatorial branch" could be a means of protecting property, while a "democratic branch" could be a means of securing personal liberty.

Implicitly the Federal Farmer suggests that the Senate under the Constitution should have a degree of stability that was not to be expected of the House of Representatives. On the other hand, there is certainly nothing in his letters that suggests that he wanted the Senate to be a bastion of conservatism. He was much too fearful of factious combinations among senators to want to see them become an entrenched body, with infrequent changes of senatorial seats. Whereas the Constitution as it stood provided that senators would have terms of six years duration, he proposed in his eleventh letter that senatorial terms be limited to three or four years. He also proposed in this letter that senators be made subject to recall by their respective states and that their seats be rotated in accordance with a prescribed schedule of rotation.

That the Constitution, if adopted as it stood, would give the Senate too much control over the executive branch of government is a major theme of the last part of the eleventh letter and the thirteenth letter. The Federal Farmer concedes that there should be some check on the president's exercise of authority in the field of foreign affairs and that it is probably safer to vest such a check in the Senate than it would be to vest it in some other organ of government. Thus, somewhat reluctantly, he approves of the requirement in Article II of the Constitution that treaties negotiated by the president must receive the consent of two-thirds of the Senate before they can have validity and also approves of giving the Senate a check on the exercise by the president of appointive power in the field of foreign affairs. On the other hand, he finds particularly objectionable the requirement in the same article that major presidential appointments in the field of domestic affairs be subject to Senate confirmation. He argues that the Senate as a council of appointment will be too large for its members to be expected to feel any degree of responsibility for actions they take in connection with appointments and goes on to insist that the Senate in such a role will not merely advise but "dictate" to the president. Especially was the Federal Farmer impressed by the corruption that so often attends the making of appointments to public office, and he assumed that senators would inevitably be involved in such corruption if they were given the authority over appointments the Constitution specified for them. In place of the Senate, the "executive council" proposed by the Federal Farmer in his thirteenth letter would share appointive power with the president in the field of domestic affairs. Because of the council's relatively small size, and because of the fact that the council would not be involved in the business of legislation, it would, according to the Federal Farmer, be a much more appropriate organ than the Senate to check on the exercise by the president of his appointive power in the field of domestic affairs.

Consistent with his general position, the Federal Farmer, in discussing the provisions of the judiciary article, concentrates largely on the situation in which the provisions leave the humble citizen. He professes to believe that certain of the traditional common law rights are left insecure, noting that jury trial is not guaranteed in civil cases[46] and that trial by jury of the vicinage is not guaranteed in criminal cases. On the question of what is actually to be expected from the proposed new federal judiciary if the Constitution is adopted without change, his position is exactly the opposite of that of Hamilton. Hamilton states in Number 78 of *The Federalist* that the judiciary is "beyond comparison the weakest" of the three principal branches of the proposed new government and goes on to say that "the general liberty of the people can never be endangered from that quarter." In the same number, he argues that the judiciary of a republic is an "excellent barrier to the encroachments and oppressions of the representative body."[47] On the other hand, the Federal Farmer contends in his fifteenth letter that the "seeds of arbitrary government" are more likely to be sown in the judiciary than in any other branch of the new system. Noting that courts have a tendency to develop "rigid systems" of law which as time goes on become "more severe and arbitrary," he suggests that "popular legislatures" are in the long run more to be depended upon than courts to live up to the requirements of strict justice.

Quite obviously the Federal Farmer is against the idea that a judicial office should be regarded as particularly sacrosant, or the idea that judges should constitute a specially privileged class. He professes not to be opposed to the idea of an independent judiciary, but he would make it constitutionally possible to reduce the salaries of judges during a period of currency deflation, with the proviso only that any such reduction must have the consent of Congress.

The desirability of a bill of rights is the chief subject of Letter XVI, and it also receives some emphasis in other letters. A general bill of rights that would include the traditional common law rights in judicial proceedings, that would give protection to citizens in reference to such matters as the quartering of troops in private residences, and that would guarantee a free press, was, according to the Federal Farmer, made extremely necessary by the broad grant of powers contemplated by the Constitution for the general government.

The Federal Constitutional Convention of 1787 had given very little attention to the subject of a bill of rights. The subject was not taken up by the Convention until five days before the Convention's adjournment, when George Mason proposed that a bill of rights be added to the Constitution. His proposal was soon voted down, no delegation supporting it.[48] Later, supporters of the Constitution took the position that a bill of rights would not be necessary and some of them argued that inclusion in the document of a bill of rights would even be a threat to human liberty. It was argued that allowing the Constitution to stand as it came from the Philadelphia Convention would make it clear that the new government was intended to be limited to the powers delegated to it. In addition, it was insisted that the enumeration in the document of rights of individuals would easily lead to the inference that what was not prohibited by the enumeration was permitted. James Madison asked in the Virginia Ratifying Convention if the enumeration of rights wouldn't imply that "everything omitted [was] given to the general government."[49] The argument took no notice of the fact that the Constitution as it stood really contained a limited enumeration of the rights of individuals, including the right to the writ of *habeas corpus,* prohibitions against bills of attainder and *ex post facto* laws, and the guarantee of jury trials in felony cases.[50]

In response to this general argument, the Federal Farmer appropriately draws attention to the numerous disputes that occur over the rights of individuals, and he insists that because of such disputes it becomes imperative that these rights be defined in law. He makes clear that he considers many of man's rights to be natural but insists that the existence of natural rights is in itself no guarantee of freedom. Doubtless he would find much support today for his argument in his sixteenth letter that the cause of individual rights is furthered by their repeated assertion, including their enumeration in constitutions.

VI

The Federal Farmer's letters merit our attention today because they constitute some of the most significant of the literature on the United States Constitution to be published during the ratification controversy. It would be too much to say that they deserve the high rating that is customarily given the essays comprising *The Federalist*. Written in haste, they do not have the graceful style of *The Federalist*. In some letters, the author is discursive, and there is a substantial amount of repetition from one letter to another. The author did not have the patience for the kind of painstaking analysis that is evidenced by James Madison in the latter's *Federalist* essays. Nevertheless, his letters reveal an extraordinarily perceptive mind. Not only was he acquainted with some of the most distinguished political and legal thinkers of the modern era of history, but he had a keen understanding of practical politics. He possessed considerable knowledge of political institutions of states in the American union and was well informed on the content of the proposed Constitution. Finally, he was consistently loyal to the political principles of the American Revolution. His theory of representation might have serious shortcomings, especially when it is applied to a country with a growing population. But he must be regarded as an outstanding defender of the right of ordinary people to participate in the political process. His assumption that men everywhere are selfish and his stress on the idea that there is a need in government to maintain a balance between social classes or orders suggest that his faith in the capacity of people to subordinate their private interests to the public good was not unbounded. On the other hand, he did not share the fear of "the democratic part" of society that was so frequently expressed by supporters of the Constitution. With him it was never a majority but always a self-serving minority of the citizen population that posed a threat of tyranny.[51]

One can find both favorable and unfavorable comments about the letters among writings of contemporaries of the Federal Farmer, and it is noteworthy that some of the more sober minds of the period were on the whole favorable. The unsigned review of the letters which appeared in *The American Magazine* in May, 1788, was critical of the Federal Farmer's writing style and of his views on representation. But the author of the review commented that the Federal Farmer's work on the whole had been conducted with "more candor and good sense than most of the publications against the new Constitution."[52] A similar judgment was expressed by Alexander Hamilton, who seems clearly to have considered the Federal Farmer to be an able adversary. He referred to the Federal Farmer by name once in *The Federalist* and once in the New York Ratifying Convention, in which Hamilton was a delegate. In the New York Convention, he rejected the "image" of aristocracy represented in the Federal Farmer's letters, branding this image as a "phantom" and as "ridiculous."[53] But in the sixty-eighth essay of *The Federalist,* Hamilton declares the Federal Farmer to be "the most plausible" of the opponents of the Constitution to have appeared in print. Here Hamilton is commenting on the Constitution's provisions for electing the United States president, and he notes that the Federal Farmer has admitted that the election has been pretty well guarded.[54]

Other Federalist comments on the letters were far from laudatory. The open letter addressed by "New England" in the *Connecticut Courant* in December, 1787, to Richard Henry Lee as author of the Federal Farmer's letters is devoted more to a personal attack on Lee than to critical appraisal of the Federal Farmer's ideas. But these ideas are referred to as "distorted and erroneous," particularly as they relate to powers vested in the Senate and judiciary.[55] A very caustic criticism of the letters came from Timothy Pickering, who was to be a prominent member of the Federalist political party during Hamilton's period as the party's chief leader, and who, like Hamilton, was to serve in President Washington's cabinet. In a long letter devoted mainly to the Federal Farmer's first pamphlet, Pickering accused the Federal Farmer of being guilty of sophistry and disingenuity. He argued that the Federal Farmer, notwithstanding his pen name, did not wish to see a "good federal government" established in the United States.[56]

Published within a little more than a month and a half after the adjournment of the Federal Constitutional Convention, the first five of the Federal Farmer's letters were in good time to be of importance in mobilizing sentiment against the Constitution, and it might well have been that the caustic comments of "New England" and Pickering were prompted by fears of the influence the letters were having or might have. Not only were both of the Federal Farmer's pamphlets repeatedly advertised in the *New York Journal,* but some of his letters were also given publicity in other newspapers. The first five letters were printed in full in the *Country Journal and Poughkeepsie Advertiser* (New York) between November 14, 1787, and January 2, 1788.

That the letters had a substantial impact on the ratification debates and actually supplied many of the arguments put forth by other opponents of the Constitution is supported by several scholars who have had occasion to study the literature of the ratification controversy.[57] Morton Borden states in his *Antifederalists Papers* that the Federal Farmer was "without a doubt the best known and most frequently read Antifederalist writer."[58] Edmund C.

Burnett, editor of the published letters of members of the Continental Congress, states that the Federal Farmer's letters became a sort of textbook for the opposition to the Constitution as *The Federalist* became for the supporters of the document.[59] Finally, Cecelia M. Kenyon says in her collection of Antifederalist writings that the first five of the Federal Farmer's letters were influential in "helping to articulate reasons for opposition to the Constitution."[60]

The letters, of course, did not achieve the author's chief objective, since that objective was to secure amendments to the Constitution before the document was finally adopted. This, however, does not mean that the letters were without significant impact on American political thought or practice. Surely the liberal and egalitarian principles of the American Revolution gained something in vitality as a result of the emphasis given them in the letters and in writings of others who opposed adoption of the Constitution as it came from the Federal Constitutional Convention. These are what the Federal Farmer meant by "the true republican principles." The last of his letters ends on the optimistic note that the debates taking place on the Constitution will make clear that the true republican principles are still alive and formidable in the United States, and he expresses the conviction that this will have a salutary effect on the operation of the proposed government if it is actually established, regardless of what might happen to proposals for constitutional amendment. He anticipated that the demonstrated vitality of the principles would have a restraining influence on persons who might be disposed to make an improper use of the new government. Undoubtedly the principles have had in many ways a restraining influence on persons in positions of authority. They provide the ideological basis of the federal Bill of Rights and are clearly manifested in the democratic sentiment of the Jeffersonian era and later times. The people's representation in the United States House of Representatives may never have been as fair for all groups as the Federal Farmer would have liked. Nevertheless, on its two-hundredth anniversary, the Republic is far from being under the kind of elite rule that he feared. In the long run, what has proved most significant has not been the mechanics of government that concerned him but the general principles to which he subscribed.

NOTES

1. *Journals of the Continental Congress, 1774–1789,* ed. Roscoe R. Hill (Washington, D.C.: Library of Congress, 1936), XXXIII, 487–503, 549.

2. *Letters of Members of the Continental Congress,* ed. Edmund C. Burnett (Washington, D.C.: Carnegie Institute of Washington, 8 vols., 1923–36), VIII, 648–49.

3. *New York Journal,* November and December, 1787; January, February, May, June, and July, 1788.

4. *Connecticut Courant,* December 24, 1787.

5. Gordon S. Wood, "The Authorship of the *Letters from the Federal Farmer*," *William and Mary Quarterly*, 3rd Ser., XXXI, No. 2 (April, 1974), 299–308.

That Lee was not the author of the Federal Farmer's pamphlets was asserted by William W. Crosskey in his *Politics and the Constitution* (Chicago: University of Chicago Press, 2 vols., 1953), II, 1300, and more was promised on this subject in a later volume of this work. However, Crosskey died in 1968 and a later volume of the work was never published.

6. *Letters of Members of the Continental Congress*, VIII, 647–49; Lee to George Mason, Oct. 1, 1787, in *The Letters of Richard Henry Lee*, ed. James Curtis Ballagh (New York: The Macmillan Company, 2 vols., 1912–14), II, 438–39.

7. Lee to Mason, Oct. 1, 1787; to Samuel Adams, Oct. 5, 1787; to George Washington, Oct. 11, 1787, in *The Letters of Richard Henry Lee*, II, 439, 447, 449; Lee to Edmund Randolph, Oct. 16, 1787, in *American Museum*, II (1787), 556.

8. Lee to George Mason, May 7, 1788; to Edmund Pendleton, May 22, 1788, in *The Letters of Richard Henry Lee*, II, 468, 472–73.

9. *The Letters of Richard Henry Lee*, II, 439. See also Lee to Samuel Adams, Oct. 5, 1787; to George Washington, Oct. 11, 1787, in ibid., II, 447, 449; and Lee to Edmund Randolph, Oct. 16, 1787, in *American Museum*, II (1787), 556.

10. See Bernard Bailyn, *The Ideological Origins of the American Revolution* (Cambridge, Mass.: Harvard University Press, 1967), 26–31.

11. Richard Henry Lee to Arthur Lee, Dec. 20, 1766; to Samuel Adams, Oct. 5, 1787, in *The Letters of Richard Henry Lee*, I, 20; II, 446, 458; to Edmund Randolph, Oct. 16, 1787, in *American Museum*, II (1787), 554, 555.

12. See, for example, Letters VII, VIII, XII, and XV of the *Federal Farmer's Letters*.

13. For evidence of the influence of the concept of the mixed constitution on Lee's thought during the Revolutionary era, see Richard Henry Lee to Arthur Lee, Dec. 20, 1766; to Edmund Pendleton, May 12, 1776, in *The Letters of Richard Henry Lee*, I, 19, 190–91. For evidence of the influence of the concept on the Federal Farmer, see especially his eleventh letter. On the ancient origin of the concept, see Kurt von Fritz, *Theory of the Mixed Constitution in Antiquity: A Critical Analysis of Polybius' Political Ideas* (New York: Columbia University Press, 1954). On the general impact of the concept on eighteenth-century American thought, see Bailyn, *Ideological Origins of the American Revolution*, 273–301, and Gordon S. Wood, *The Creation of the American Republic, 1776–1789* (Chapel Hill, N.C.: University of North Carolina Press, 1969), Chap. VI.

14. *American Bibliography*, ed. Charles Evans (Chicago: Columbia Press, 1903–55), VII, No. 20456.

15. On weather conditions during the winter of 1788, see Lee to———, April 28, 1788, in *The Letters of Richard Henry Lee*, II, 463–64. On Lee's plans for his departure from New York for Virginia during the fall of 1787 see Lee to Samuel Adams, Oct. 5 and Oct. 27, 1788; to George Washington, Oct. 11, in ibid., II, 447, 458, 550.

16. The letter as made public, with a postscript containing the proposals for amendment to the Constitution presented by Lee to Congress, is printed in the *American Museum*, II (1787), 553–58.

17. Wood, "The Authorship of the *Letters from the Federal Farmer*," *William and Mary Quarterly*, 3rd Ser., XXXI, No. 2, 301–03.

18. *Records of the Federal Constitutional Convention of 1787*, ed. Max Farrand (New Haven, Conn.: Yale University Press, 3 vols., 1911), I, 20.

19. Edmund Randolph, *Letter on the Federal Constitution,* pp. 10, 13. In *Pamphlets on the Constitution of the United States,* ed. Paul Leicester Ford (Brooklyn, N.Y., 1888). For comments on Randolph's equivocal position on the Constitution, see ibid., 1.

20. Lee to William Whipple, July 1, 1783; to Samuel Adams, March 14, 1785; to James Madison, Aug. 11, 1785, in *The Letters of Richard Henry Lee,* II, 284, 344, 383.

21. Richard Henry Lee to Francis Lightfoot Lee, July 14, 1787; to John Adams, Sept. 5, 1787, in ibid., II, 424, 434.

22. Lee to George Mason, May 15, 1787, in ibid., II, 421.

23. Lee to Mason, Oct. 1, 1787; to Pendleton, May 22, 1788, in ibid., II, 438, 473; to Randolph, Oct. 16, 1787, in *American Museum,* II, 555–56, 558.

24. See Lee's proposals to Congress as printed in *The Letters of Richard Henry Lee,* II, 443n, and *Letters of Members of the Continental Congress,* VIII, 649.

25. Lee to Adams, Oct. 27, 1787; to Mason, May 7, 1788, in *The Letters of Richard Henry Lee,* II, 456–58, 466–69. On the general harmony between Adams' political views and those of Lee, see Crosskey, *Politics and the Constitution,* II, 1300. On the harmony of Mason's views with those of Lee, see George Washington to James Madison, Oct. 10, 1787, in George Washington, *Writings of,* ed. John C. Fitzpatrick (Washington: United States Government Printing Office, 39 vols., 1931–44). XXIX, 285. Washington comments here that the tenets of Mason and Lee are "always in unison."

If there was anything in Lee's correspondence or in other family papers that might suggest that he was the author of the Federal Farmer's letters, presumably his first biographer, who was also a grandson of his, was unaware of it, as he makes no mention of the matter. See Richard Henry Lee, *Memoir of the Life of Richard Henry Lee and His Correspondence with the Most Distinguished Men in America and Europe* (Philadelphia: H.C. Carey and I. Lea, 2 vols., 1825).

26. See Walter H. Bennett, *American Theories of Federalism* (University, Alabama: The University of Alabama Press, 1964), 59–63, and Martin Diamond, "What the Framers Meant by Federalism," in *A Nation of States: Essays on the American Federal System,* ed. Robert A. Goldwin (Chicago: Rand McNally and Company, 1963), 26–30.

27. Bennett, *American Theories of Federalism,* 63–66, 77.

28. Baron de Montesquieu, *The Spirit of the Laws.* Trans. Thomas Nugent (New York and London: Hafner Publishing Company, 2 vols., 1966), I, Bk. VIII, Chaps. 16, 20. For Montesquieu's views on the superiority of a "confederate" republic to a large republic that is not federal or confederate, see Bk. IX, Chap. 1.

29. See especially Letters I and II. Although the Federal Farmer writes specifically of the disadvantages of "extensive republics," from his letters as a whole it becomes clear that he does not consider federal republics which happen to be large as being under the same disadvantages as extensive republics that are not federal. In leaving a large portion of the public business to member states or provinces, a federal republic avoided many of the difficulties that were inevitably encountered by large republics that were not federal.

30. The Constitution provides in Article I, Sec. 4, that "the times, places and manner of holding elections for senators and representatives, shall be prescribed in

each state by the legislature thereof" but that "the Congress may at any time make or alter such regulations, except as to the place of chusing senators."

31. Article I, Sec. 2.

32. Ibid.

33. Alexander Hamilton, James Madison, and John Jay, *The Federalists,* ed. Benjamin Fletcher Wright (Cambridge, Mass.: Belknap Press of Harvard University Press,1966), No. 10, 129–32.

34. John Adams, *Works of,* ed. Charles Francis Adams (Boston: Charles C. Little and James Brown, 10 vols., 1850–56), IV, 195, 205.

35. *The Works of the Honorable Edmund Burke,* 9 vols. (London: Henry G. Bohn, 1845), I, 395.

36. Ibid., II, 12–13.

37. The utilitarian theory of representation is probably best elaborated by James Mill, himself a leading utilitarian. See his *Essay on Government* (Cambridge, England: At the University Press, 1937), especially Chap. VII.

38. On the various plans of "proportional representation" that have been popular in the nineteenth and twentieth centuries, see Clarence Gilbert Hoag and George Hervey Hallet, Jr., *Proportional Representation* (New York: The Macmillan Company, 1926). An example of proposals for "functional representation" is furnished by G.D.H. Cole's *Social Theory* (New York: Frederick A. Stokes Company, 1920). Cole argues that churches, business associations, trade unions, farmers' co-operatives, etc. constitute a better basis for representing the people's real interests and views than territorial districts. See Chap. VI.

39. Data on the size of the House membership after the various decennial censuses taken since 1790 are contained in the *Congressional Directory,* 94th Congress, First Session (Washington, D.C.: United States Government Printing Office, 1975), 414.

40. *The Federalist,* No. 35, 256–57.

41. Ibid., No. 55, 375; No. 58, 392.

42. Ibid., No. 57, 384–85.

43. Ibid., No. 10, 134–35.

44. Ibid., No. 35, 258.

45. Ibid., No. 10, 134; No. 58, 392.

46. The guarantee was added later, being included in the Seventh Amendment to the Constitution.

47. *The Federalist,* No. 78, 490–91.

48. *Records of the Federal Constitutional Convention of 1787,* II, 587–88.

49. *The Debates in the Several State Conventions on the Adoption of the Federal Constitution as Recommended by the General Convention in Philadelphia in 1787,* 2nd edition, ed. Jonathan Elliot (Philadelphia: J.B. Lippincott Company, 5 vols., 1836), III, 620.

50. Article I, Secs. 9 and 10; Article III, Sec. 2.

51. That the Antifederalists as a group had a great deal of faith in the people is a conclusion reached by Wood, *The Creation of the American Republic,* 516, 520, and Robert Allen Rutland, *The Ordeal of the Constitution: The Antifederalists in the Ratification Struggle of 1787–1788* (Norman, Okla.: University of Oklahoma Press, 1966), 312, 314. A directly opposite view is represented by Cecelia M. Kenyon, "Men of Little Faith: The Antifederalists and the Nature of Representative Government," *William and Mary Quarterly,* 3rd Ser., XII (Jan., 1955), 42–43.

52. *The American Magazine,* May, 1788, 422–23.

53. Elliot, *Debates,* II, 256.

54. *The Federalist,* No. 68, 440.

55. "New England," *pseud.,* to Richard Henry Lee, *Connecticut Courant,* Dec. 24, 1787.

56. Timothy Pickering to Charles Tillinghast, Dec. 24, 1787, in Octavius Pickering and Charles W. Upham, *The Life of Timothy Pickering,* 4 vols., (Boston: Little, Brown, and Company, 1867–73), II, 352–68.

57. A detailed analysis of arguments against the Constitution as set forth by those who opposed its ratification is contained in Jackson Turner Main, *The Antifederalists* (Chapel Hill, N.C.: University of North Carolina Press, 1961), Chaps. VI and VII.

58. *The Antifederalist Papers,* ed. Morton Borden (Michigan State University Press, 1965), 95.

59. *Letters of Members of the Continental Congress,* VIII, xlix.

60. *The Antifederalists,* ed. Cecelia M. Kenyon (Indianapolis: The Bobbs-Merrill Company, 1966), 197.

THE
FEDERAL FARMER'S
FIRST PAMPHLET

OBSERVATIONS

LEADING to a FAIR EXAMINATION

OF THE

SYSTEM of GOVERNMENT,

PROPOSED BY THE LATE

CONVENTION;

AND TO SEVERAL ESSENTIAL AND NECES-
SARY ALTERATIONS IN IT.

IN A NUMBER OF

LETTERS

FROM THE

FEDERAL FARMER TO THE REPUBLICAN.

Lee, Richard Henry,

◅◅◅◅◅◅◅◅◅◅◅►►►►►►►►►►

New-York

PRINTED IN THE YEAR M,DCC,LXXXVII.

TITLE PAGE OF THE FEDERAL FARMER'S
FIRST PAMPHLET, CONTAINING LETTERS I–V
(COURTESY OF THE LIBRARY OF CONGRESS)

I

Introduction

DEAR SIR,

MY letters to you last winter, on the subject of a well balanced national government for the United States, were the result of free
enquiry; when I passed from that subject to enquiries relative to our commerce, revenues, past administration, &c. I anticipated the anxieties I feel, on
carefully examining the plan of government proposed by the convention. It
appears to be a plan retaining some federal features; but to be the first
important step, and to aim strongly to one consolidated government of the
United States. It leaves the powers of government, and the representation of
the people, so unnaturally divided between the general and state governments, that the operations of our system must be very uncertain. My uniform
federal attachments, and the interest I have in the protection of property, and
a steady execution of the laws, will convince you, that, if I am under any biass
at all, it is in favor of any general system which shall promise those advantages. The instability of our laws increases my wishes for firm and steady
government; but then, I can consent to no government, which, in my opinion, is not calculated equally to preserve the rights of all orders of men in the
community. My object has been to join with those who have endeavoured to
supply the defects in the forms of our governments by a steady and proper
administration of them. Though I have long apprehended that fraudulent
debtors, and embarrassed men, on the one hand, and men, on the other,
unfriendly to republican equality, would produce an uneasiness among the
people, and prepare the way, not for cool and deliberate reforms in the
governments, but for changes calculated to promote the interests of particular orders of men. Acquit me, sir, of any agency in the formation of the new
system; I shall be satisfied with seeing, if it shall be adopted, a prudent
administration. Indeed I am so much convinced of the truth of Pope's maxim,
that "That which is best administered is best," that I am much inclined to
subscribe to it from experience. I am not disposed to unreasonably contend
about forms. I know our situation is critical, and it behoves us to make the
best of it. A federal government of some sort is necessary. We have suffered
the present to languish; and whether the confederation was capable or not
originally of answering any valuable purposes, it is now but of little impor-

tance. I will pass by the men, and states, who have been particularly instrumental in preparing the way for a change, and, perhaps, for governments not very favourable to the people at large. A constitution is now presented which we may reject, or which we may accept, with or without amendments; and to which point we ought to direct our exertions, is the question. To determine this question, with propriety, we must attentively examine the system itself, and the probable consequences of either step. This I shall endeavour to do, so far as I am able, with candor and fairness; and leave you to decide upon the propriety of my opinions, the weight of my reasons, and how far my conclusions are well drawn. Whatever may be the conduct of others, on the present occasion, I do not mean, hastily and positively to decide on the merits of the constitution proposed. I shall be open to conviction, and always disposed to adopt that which, all things considered, shall appear to me to be most for the happiness of the community. It must be granted, that if men hastily and blindly adopt a system of government, they will as hastily and as blindly be led to alter or abolish it; and changes must ensue, one after another, till the peaceable and better part of the community will grow weary with changes, tumults and disorders, and be disposed to accept any government, however despotic, that shall promise stability and firmness.

The first principal question that occurs is, Whether, considering our situation, we ought to precipitate the adoption of the proposed constitution? If we remain cool and temperate, we are in no immediate danger of any commotions; we are in a state of perfect peace, and in no danger of invasions; the state governments are in the full exercise of their powers; and our governments answer all present exigencies, except the regulation of trade, securing credit, in some cases, and providing for the interest, in some instances, of the public debts; and whether we adopt a change three or nine months hence, can make but little odds with the private circumstances of individuals; their happiness and prosperity, after all, depend principally upon their own exertions. We are hardly recovered from a long and distressing war: The farmers, fishermen, &c, have not yet fully repaired the waste made by it. Industry and frugality are again assuming their proper station. Private debts are lessened, and public debts incurred by the war have been, by various ways, diminished; and the public lands have now become a productive source for diminishing them much more. I know uneasy men, who wish very much to precipitate, do not admit all these facts; but they are facts well known to all men who are thoroughly informed in the affairs of this country. It must, however, be admitted, that our federal system is defective, and that some of the state governments are not well administered; but, then, we impute to the defects in our governments many evils and embarrassments which are most clearly the result of the late war. We must allow men to conduct on the present occasion, as on all similar ones. They will urge a thousand pretences to answer their purposes on both sides. When we want a man to change his condition, we describe it as miserable, wretched, and despised; and draw a pleasing picture of that which we would have him assume. And when we wish the contrary, we reverse our descriptions. Whenever a clamor is raised, and idle men get to work, it is highly necessary to examine facts carefully, and without unreasonably suspecting men of falsehood, to examine, and enquire attentively, under what impressions they act. It is too often the case in political concerns, that men state facts not as they are, but as they wish them to be; and almost every man, by calling to mind past scenes, will find this to be true.

Nothing but the passions of ambitious, impatient, or disorderly men, I conceive, will plunge us into commotions, if time should be taken fully to examine and consider the system proposed. Men who feel easy in their circumstances, and such as are not sanguine in their expectations relative to the consequences of the proposed change, will remain quiet under the existing governments. Many commercial and monied men, who are uneasy, not without just cause, ought to be respected; and, by no means, unreasonably disappointed in their expectations and hopes; but as to those who expect employments under the new constitution; as to those weak and ardent men who always expect to be gainers by revolutions, and whose lot it generally is to get out of one difficulty into another, they are very little to be regarded: and as to those who designedly avail themselves of this weakness and ardor, they are to be despised. It is natural for men, who wish to hasten the adoption of a measure, to tell us, now is the crisis—now is the critical moment which must be seized, or all will be lost: and to shut the door against free enquiry, whenever conscious the thing presented has defects in it, which time and investigation will probably discover. This has been the custom of tyrants and their dependants in all ages. If it is true, what has been so often said, that the people of this country cannot change their condition for the worse, I presume it still behoves them to endeavour deliberately to change it for the better. The fickle and ardent, in any community, are the proper tools for establishing despotic government. But it is deliberate and thinking men, who must establish and secure governments on free principles. Before they decide on the plan proposed, they will enquire whether it will probably be a blessing or a curse to this people.

The present moment discovers a new face in our affairs. Our object has been all along, to reform our federal system, and to strengthen our governments—to establish peace, order and justice in the community—but a new object now presents. The plan of government now proposed is evidently calculated totally to change, in time, our condition as a people. Instead of being thirteen republics, under a federal head, it is clearly designed to make us one consolidated government. Of this, I think, I shall fully convince you, in my following letters on this subject. This consolidation of the states has been the object of several men in this country for some time past. Whether such a change can ever be effected in any manner; whether it can be effected without convulsions and civil wars: whether such a change will not totally destroy the liberties of this country—time only can determine.

To have a just idea of the government before us, and to shew that a consolidated one is the object in view, it is necessary not only to examine the plan, but also its history, and the politics of its particular friends.

The confederation was formed when great confidence was placed in the voluntary exertions of individuals, and of the respective states; and the framers of it, to guard against usurpation, so limited and checked the powers, that, in many respects, they are inadequate to the exigencies of the union. We find, therefore, members of congress urging alterations in the federal system almost as soon as it was adopted. It was early proposed to vest congress with powers to levy an impost, to regulate trade, &c. but such was known to be the caution of the states in parting with power, that the vestment, even of these, was proposed to be under several checks and limitations. During the war, the general confusion, and the introduction of paper money, infused in the minds of people vague ideas respecting government and credit. We expected too much from the return of peace, and of course we have been disappointed. Our governments have been new and unsettled; and several legislatures, by making tender, suspension, and paper money laws, have given just cause of uneasiness to creditors. By these and other causes, several orders of men in the community have been prepared, by degrees, for a change of government; and this very abuse of power in the legislatures, which, in some cases, has been charged upon the democratic part of the community, has furnished aristocratical men with those very weapons, and those very means, with which, in great measure, they are rapidly effecting their favourite object. And should an oppressive government be the consequence of the proposed change, posterity may reproach not only a few overbearing unprincipled men, but those parties in the states which have misused their powers.

The conduct of several legislatures, touching paper money, and tender laws, has prepared many honest men for changes in government, which otherwise they would not have thought of—when by the evils, on the one hand, and by the secret instigations of artful men, on the other, the minds of men were become sufficiently uneasy, a bold step was taken, which is usually followed by a revolution, or a civil war. A general convention for mere commercial purposes was moved for—the authors of this measure saw that the people's attention was turned solely to the amendment of the federal system; and that, had the idea of a total change been started, probably no state would have appointed members to the convention. The idea of destroying, ultimately, the state government, and forming one consolidated system, could not have been admitted—a convention, therefore, merely for vesting in congress power to regulate trade was proposed. This was pleasing to the commercial towns; and the landed people had little or no concern about it. September, 1786, a few men from the middle states met at Annapolis, and hastily proposed a convention to be held in May, 1787, for the purpose, generally, of amending the confederation—this was done before the delegates of Massachusetts, and of the other states arrived—still not a word was said about destroying the old constitution, and making a new one—The states still unsuspecting, and not aware that they were passing the Rubicon, appointed members to the new convention, for the sole and express purpose of revising and amending the confederation—and, probably, not one man in ten thousand in the United States, till within these ten or twelve days, had an idea that the old ship was to be destroyed, and he put to the alternative of embarking in the new ship presented, or of being left in danger of sinking— The States, I believe, universally supposed the convention would report alterations in the confederation, which would pass an examination in congress, and after being agreed to there, would be confirmed by all the legislatures, or be rejected. Virginia made a very respectable appointment, and placed at the head of it the first man in America: In this appointment there was a mixture of political characters; but Pennsylvania appointed principally those men who are esteemed aristocratical. Here the favorite moment for changing the government was evidently discerned by a few men, who seized it with address. Ten other states appointed, and tho' they chose men principally connected with commerce and the judicial department yet they appointed many good republican characters—had they all attended we should now see, I am persuaded, a better system presented. The non attendance of eight or nine men, who were appointed members of the convention, I shall ever consider as a very unfortunate event to the United States.—Had they attended, I am pretty clear that the result of the convention would not have had that strong tendency to aristocracy now discernable in every part of the plan. There would not have been so great an accumulation of powers especially as to the internal police of the country, in a few hands, as the constitution reported proposes to vest in them—the young visionary men, and the consolidating aristocracy, would have been more restrained than they have been. Eleven states met in the convention, and after four months close attention presented the new constitution, to be adopted or rejected by the people. The uneasy and fickle part of the community may be prepared to receive any form of government; but, I presume, the enlightened and substantial part will give any constitution presented for their adoption, a candid and thorough examination; and silence those designing or empty men, who weakly and rashly attempt to precipitate the adoption of a system of so much importance—We shall view the convention with proper respect—and, at the same time that we reflect there were men of abilities and integrity in it, we must recollect how disproportionably the democratic and aristocratic parts of the community were represented—Perhaps the judicious friends and opposers of the new constitution will agree, that it is best to let it rest solely on its own merits, or be condemned for its own defects.

In the first place, I shall premise, that the plan proposed is a plan of accommodation—and that it is in this way only, and by giving up a part of our opinions, that we can ever expect to obtain a government founded in freedom and compact. This circumstance candid men will always keep in view, in the discussion of this subject.

The plan proposed appears to be partly federal, but principally however, calculated ultimately to make the states one consolidated government.

The first interesting question, therefore suggested, is, how far the states can be consolidated into one entire government on free principles. In considering this question extensive objects are to be taken into view, and important changes in the forms of government to be carefully attended to in all their consequences. The happiness of the people at large must be the great object with every honest statesman, and he will direct every movement to this point. If we are so situated as a people, as not to be able to enjoy equal happiness and advantages under one government, the consolidation of the states cannot be admitted.

There are three different forms of free government under which the United States may exist as one nation; and now is, perhaps, the time to determine to which we will direct our views. 1. Distinct republics connected under a federal head. In this case the respective state governments must be the principal guardians of the people's rights, and exclusively regulate their internal police; in them must rest the balance of government. The congress of the states, or federal head, must consist of delegates amendable to, and removable by the respective states: This congress must have general directing powers; powers to require men and monies of the states; to make treaties; peace and war; to direct the operations of armies, &c. Under this federal modification of government, the powers of congress would be rather advisory or recommendatory than coercive. 2. We may do away with the several state governments, and form or consolidate all the states into one entire government, with one executive, one judiciary, and one legislature, consisting of senators and representatives collected from all parts of the union: In this case there would be a compleat consolidation of the states. 3. We may consolidate the states as to certain national objects, and leave them severally distinct independent republics, as to internal police generally. Let the general government consist of an executive, a judiciary, and balanced legislature, and its powers extend exclusively to all foreign concerns, causes arising on the seas, to commerce, imports, armies, navies, Indian affairs, peace and war, and to a few internal concerns of the community; to the coin, post-offices, weights and measures, a general plan for the militia, to naturalization, *and, perhaps to bankruptcies,* leaving the internal police of the community, in other respects, exclusively to the state governments; as the administration of justice in all causes arising internally, the laying and collecting of internal taxes, and the forming of the militia according to a general plan prescribed. In this case there would be a compleat consolidation, *quoad* certain objects only.

Touching the first, or federal plan, I do not think much can be said in its favor: The sovereignity of the nation, without coercive and efficient powers to collect the strength of it, cannot always be depended on to answer the purposes of government, and in a congress of representatives of sovereign states, there must necessarily be an unreasonable mixture of powers in the same hands.

As to the second, or compleat consolidating plan, it deserves to be carefully considered at this time, by every American: If it be impracticable, it is a fatal error to model our governments, directing our views ultimately to it.

The third plan, or partial consolidation, is, in my opinion, the only one that can secure the freedom and happiness of this people. I once had some general ideas that the second plan was practicable, but from long attention, and the proceedings of the convention, I am fully satisfied, that this third plan is the only one we can with safety and propriety proceed upon. Making this the standard to point out, with candor and fairness, the parts of the new constitution which appear to be improper, is my object. The convention appears to have proposed the partial consolidation evidently with a view to collect all powers ultimately, in the United States into one entire government; and from its views in this respect, and from the tenacity of the small states to have an equal vote in the senate, probably originated the greatest defects in the proposed plan.

Independant of the opinions of many great authors, that free elective government cannot be extended over large territories, a few reflections must evince, that one government and general legislation alone, never can extend equal benefits to all parts of the United States: Different laws, customs, and opinions exist in the different states, which by a uniform system of laws would be unreasonably invaded. The United States contain about a million of square miles, and in half a century will, probably, contain ten millions of people; and from the center to the extremes is about 800 miles.

Before we do away with the state governments, or adopt measures that will tend to abolish them, and to consolidate the states into one entire government, several principles should be considered and facts ascertained:—These, and my examination into the essential parts of the proposed plan, I shall pursue in my next.

Your's, &c.
The FEDERAL FARMER.

II

Essentials of a Free Government

OCTOBER 9, 1787.

DEAR SIR,

T HE essential parts of a free and good government are a full and equal representation of the people in the legislature, and the jury trial of the vicinage in the administration of justice—a full and equal representation, is that which possesses the same interests, feelings, opinions, and views the people themselves would were they all assembled—a fair representation, therefore, should be so regulated, that every order of men in the community, according to the common course of elections, can have a share in it—in order to allow professional men, merchants, traders, farmers, mechanics, &c. to bring a just proportion of their best informed men respectively into the legislature, the representation must be considerably numerous—We have about 200 state senators in the United States, and a less number than that of federal representatives cannot, clearly, be a full representation of this people, in the affairs of internal taxation and police, were there but one legislature for the whole union. The representation cannot be equal, or the situation of the people proper for one government only—if the extreme parts of the society cannot be represented as fully as the central—It is apparently impracticable that this should be the case in this extensive country—it would be impossible to collect a representation of the parts of the country five, six, and seven hundred miles from the seat of government.

Under one general government alone, there could be but one judiciary, one supreme and a proper number of inferior courts. I think it would be totally impracticable in this case to preserve a due administration of justice, and the real benefits of the jury trial of the vicinage—there are now supreme courts in each state in the union; and a great number of county and other courts subordinate to each supreme court—most of these supreme and inferior courts are itinerant, and hold their sessions in different parts every year of their respective states, counties and districts—with all these moving courts, our citizens, from the vast extent of the country must travel very considerable distances from home to find the place where justice is administered. I am not for bringing justice so near to individuals as to afford them any temptation to engage in law suits; though I think it one of the greatest benefits in a good government, that each citizen should find a court of justice within a reasonable distance, perhaps, within a day's travel of his home; so that, without great inconveniences and enormous expences, he may have the advantages of his witnesses and jury—it would be impracticable to derive these advantages from one judiciary—the one supreme court at most could only set in the centre of the union, and move once a year into the centre of the eastern and southern extremes of it—and, in this case, each citizen, on an average, would travel 150 or 200 miles to find this court—that however inferior courts might be properly placed in the different counties, and districts of the union, the appellate jurisdiction would be intolerable and expensive.

If it were possible to consolidate the states, and preserve the features of a free government, still it is evident that the middle states, the parts of the union, about the seat of government, would enjoy great advantages, while the remote states would experience the many inconveniences of remote provinces. Wealth, offices, and the benefits of government would collect in the centre: and the extreme states, and their principal towns, become much less important.

There are other considerations which tend to prove that the idea of one consolidated whole, on free principles, is ill-founded—the laws of a free government rest on the confidence of the people, and operate gently—and never can extend their influence very far—if they are executed on free principles, about the centre, where the benefits of the government induce the people to support it voluntarily, yet they must be executed on the principles of fear and force in the extremes—This has been the case with every extensive republic of which we have any accurate account.

There are certain unalienable and fundamental rights, which in forming the social compact, ought to be explicitly ascertained and fixed—a free and enlightened people in forming this compact, will not resign all their rights to those who govern, and they will fix limits to their legislators and rulers, which will soon be plainly seen by those who are governed, as well as by those who govern: and the latter will know they cannot be passed unperceived by the former, and without giving a general alarm—These rights should be made the basis of every constitution; and if a people be so situated, or have such different opinions that they cannot agree in ascertaining and fixing them, it is a very strong argument against their attempting to form one entire society, to live under one system of laws only.—I confess, I never thought the people of these states differed essentially in these respects; they having derived all these rights from one common source, the British systems; and having in the formation of their state constitutions, discovered that their ideas relative to these rights are very similar. However, it is now said that the states differ so essentially in these respects, and even in the important article of the trial by jury, that when assembled in convention, they can agree to no words by which to establish that trial, or by which to ascertain and establish many other of these rights, as fundamental articles in the social compact. If so, we proceed to consolidate the states on no solid basis whatever.

But I do not pay much regard to the reasons given for not bottoming the new constitution on a better bill of rights. I still believe a complete federal bill of rights to be very practicable. Nevertheless I acknowledge the proceedings of the convention furnish my mind with many new and strong reasons, against a complete consolidation of the states. They tend to convince me, that it cannot be carried with propriety very far—that the convention have gone much farther in one respect than they found it practicable to go in another; that is, they propose to lodge in the general government very extensive powers—*powers* nearly, if not altogether, complete and unlimited, over the purse and the sword. But, in its organization, they furnish the strongest proof that the proper limbs, or parts of a government, to support and execute those powers on proper principles (or in which they can be safely lodged) cannot be formed. These powers must be lodged somewhere in every society; but then they should be lodged where the strength and guardians of the people are collected. They can be wielded, or safely used, in a free country only by an able executive and judiciary, a respectable senate, and a secure, full, and equal representation of the people. I think the principles I have premised or brought into view, are well founded—I think they will not be denied by any fair reasoner. It is in connection with these, and other solid principles, we are to examine the constitution. It is not a few democratic phrases, or a few well formed features, that will prove its merits; or a few small omissions that will produce its rejection among men of sense; they will enquire what are the essential powers in a community, and what are nominal ones; where and how the essential powers shall be lodged to secure government, and to secure true liberty.

In examining the proposed constitution carefully, we must clearly perceive an unnatural separation of these powers from the substantial representation of the people. The state governments will exist, with all their governors, senators, representatives, officers and expences; in these will be nineteen twentieths of the representatives of the people; they will have a near connection, and their members an immediate intercourse with the people; and the probability is, that the state governments will possess the confidence of the people, and be considered generally as their immediate guardians.

The general government will consist of a new species of executive, a small senate, and a very small house of representatives. As many citizens will be more than three hundred miles from the seat of this government as will be nearer to it, its judges and officers cannot be very numerous, without making our governments very expensive. Thus will stand the state and the general governments, should the constitution be adopted without any alterations in their organization; but as to powers, the general government will possess all essential ones, at least on paper, and those of the states a mere shadow of power. And therefore, unless the people shall make some great exertions to restore to the state governments their powers in matters of internal police; as the powers to lay and collect, exclusively, internal taxes, to govern the militia, and to hold the decisions of their own judicial courts upon their own laws final, the balance cannot possibly continue long; but the state governments must be annihilated, or continue to exist for no purpose.

It is however to be observed, that many of the essential powers given the national government are not exclusively given; and the general government may have prudence enough to forbear the exercise of those which may still be exercised by the respective states. But this cannot justify the impropriety of giving powers, the exercise of which prudent men will not attempt, and imprudent men will, or probably can, exercise only in a manner destructive of free government. The general government, organized as it is, may be adequate to many valuable objects, and be able to carry its laws into execution on proper principles in several cases; but I think its warmest friends will not contend, that it can carry all the powers proposed to be lodged in it into effect, without calling to its aid a military force, which must very soon destroy all elective governments in the country, produce anarchy, or establish despotism. Though we cannot have now a complete idea of what will be the operations of the proposed system, we may, allowing things to have their common course, have a very tolerable one. The powers lodged in the general government, if exercised by it, must intimately affect the internal police of the states, as well as external concerns; and there is no reason to expect the numerous state governments, and their connections, will be very friendly to the execution of federal laws in those internal affairs, which hitherto have been under their own immediate management. There is more reason to believe, that the general government, far removed from the people, and none of its members elected oftener than once in two years, will be forgot or neglected, and its laws in many cases disregarded, unless a multitude of officers and military force be continually kept in view, and employed to enforce the execution of the laws, and to make the government feared and respected. No position can be truer than this, That in this country either neglected laws, or a military execution of them, must lead to a revolution, and to the destruction of freedom. Neglected laws must first lead to anarchy and confusion; and a military execution of laws is only a shorter way to the same point—despotic government.

Your's, &c.
The FEDERAL FARMER.

III

Organization and Powers of the
Proposed Government I

OCTOBER 10th, 1787.

DEAR SIR,

T HE great object of a free people must be so to form their government and laws and so to administer them, as to create a confidence in, and respect for the laws; and thereby induce the sensible and virtuous part of the community to declare in favor of the laws, and to support them without an expensive military force. I wish, though I confess I have not much hope, that this may be the case with the laws of congress under the new constitution. I am fully convinced that we must organize the national government on different principles, and make the parts of it more efficient, and secure in it more effectually the different interests in the community; or else leave in the state governments some powers proposed to be lodged in it—at least till such an organization shall be found to be practicable. Not sanguine in my expectations of a good federal administration, and satisfied, as I am, of the impracticability of consolidating the states, and at the same time of preserving the rights of the people at large, I believe we ought still to leave some of those powers in the state governments, in which the people, in fact, will still be represented—to define some other powers proposed to be vested in the general government, more carefully, and to establish a few principles to secure a proper exercise of the powers given it. It is not my object to multiply objections, or to contend about inconsiderable powers or amendments; I wish the system adopted with a few alterations; but those, in my mind, are essential ones; if adopted without, every good citizen will acquiesce though I shall consider the duration of our governments, and the liberties of this people, very much dependant on the administration of the general government. A wise and honest administration, may make the people happy under any government; but necessity only can justify even our leaving open avenues to the abuse of power, by wicked, unthinking, or ambitious men. I will examine, first, the organization of the proposed government, in order to judge; 2d. with propriety, what powers are improperly, at least prematurely lodged in it. I shall examine, 3d, the undefined powers; and 4th, those powers, the exercise of which is not secured on safe and proper ground.

First. As to the organization—the house of representatives, the democrative branch, as it is called, is to consist of 65 members: that is, about one representative for fifty thousand inhabitants, to be chosen biennially—the federal legislature may increase this number to one for each thirty thousand inhabitants, abating fractional numbers in each state.—Thirty-three representatives will make a quorum for doing business, and a majority of those present determine the sense of the house.—I have no idea that the interests, feelings, and opinions of three or four millions of people, especially touching internal taxation can be collected in such a house.—In the nature of things, nine times in ten, men of the elevated classes in the community only can be chosen—Connecticut, for instance, will have five representatives—not one man in a hundred of those who form the democrative branch in the state legislature, will, on a fair computation, be one of the five—The people of this country, in one sense, may all be democratic; but if we make the proper distinction between the few men of wealth and abilities, and consider them, as we ought, as the natural aristocracy of the country, and the great body of the people, the middle and lower classes, as the democracy, this federal representative branch will have but very little democracy in it, even this small representation is not secured on proper principles.—The branches of the legislature are essential parts of the fundamental compact, and ought to be so fixed by the people, that the legislature cannot alter itself by modifying the elections of its own members. This, by a part of Art. 1. Sect. 4, the general legislature may do, it may evidently so regulate elections as to secure the choice of any particular description of men.—It may make the whole state one district—make the capital, or any places in the state, the place or places of election—it may declare that the five men (or whatever the number may be the state may chuse) who shall have the most votes shall be considered as chosen—In this case it is easy to perceive how the people who live scattered in the inland towns will bestow their votes on different men—and how a few men in a city, in any order or profession, may unite and place any five men they please highest among those that may be voted for—and all this may be done constitutionally, and by those silent operations, which are not immediately perceived by the people in general.—I know it is urged, that the general legislature will be disposed to regulate elections on fair and just principles:—This may be true—good men will generally govern well with almost any constitution: but why in laying the foundation of the social system, need we unnecessarily leave a door open to improper regulations?—This is a very general and unguarded clause, and many evils may flow from that part which authorises the congress to regulate elections—Were it omitted, the regulations of elections would be solely in the respective states, where the people are substantially represented; and where the elections ought to be regulated, otherwise to secure a representation from all parts of the community, in making the constitution, we ought to provide for dividing each state into a proper number of districts, and for confining the electors in each district to the choice of some men, who shall have a permanent interest and residence in it; and also for this essential object, that the representative elected shall have a majority of the votes of those electors who shall attend and give their votes.

In considering the practicability of having a full and equal representation of the people from all parts of the union, not only distances and different opinions, customs, and views common in extensive tracts of country, are to be taken into view, but many differences peculiar to Eastern, Middle, and Southern states. These differences are not so perceivable among the members of congress, and men of general information in the states, as among the men who would properly form the democratic branch. The Eastern states are very democratic, and composed chiefly of moderate freeholders; they have but few rich men and no slaves; the Southern states are composed chiefly of rich planters and slaves; they have but few moderate freeholders, and the prevailing influence, in them, is generally a dissipated aristocracy: The Middle states partake partly of the Eastern and partly of the Southern character.

Perhaps, nothing could be more disjointed, unweildly and incompetent to doing business with harmony and dispatch, than a federal house of representatives properly numerous for the great objects of taxation, &c. collected from the several states; whether such men would ever act in concert; whether they would not worry along a few years, and then be the means of separating the parts of the union, is very problematical?—View this system in whatever form we can, propriety brings us still to this point, a federal government possessed of general and complete powers, as to those national objects which cannot well come under the cognizance of the internal laws of the respective states, and this federal government, accordingly, consisting of branches not very numerous.

The house of representatives is on the plan of consolidation, but the senate is entirely on the federal plan; and Delaware will have as much constitutional influence in the senate, as the largest state in the union: and in this senate are lodged legislative, executive and judicial powers: Ten states in this union urge that they are small states, nine of which were present in the convention.—They were interested in collecting large powers into the hands of the senate, in which each state still will have its equal share of power. I suppose it was impracticable for the three large states, as they were called, to get the senate formed on any other principles: But this only proves, that we cannot form one general government on equal and just principles—and proves, that we ought not to lodge in it such extensive powers before we are convinced of the practicability of organizing it on just and equal principles. The senate will consist of two members from each state, chosen by the state legislatures, every sixth year. The clause referred to, respecting the elections of representatives, empowers the general legislature to regulate the elections of senators also, "except as to the places of chusing senators."—There is, therefore, but little more security in the elections than in those of representatives: Fourteen senators make a quorum for business, and a majority of the senators present give the vote of the senate, except in giving judgment upon an impeachment, or in making treaties, or in expelling a member, when two-thirds of the senators present must agree—The members of the legislature are not excluded from being elected to any military offices, or any civil offices, except those created, or the emoluments of which shall be increased by themselves: two-thirds of the members present, of either house, may expel a member at pleasure. The senate is an independant branch of the legislature, a court for trying impeachments, and also a part of the executive, having a negative in the making of all treaties, and in appointing almost all officers.

The vice president is not a very important, if not an unnecessary part of the system—he may be a part of the senate at one period, and act as the supreme executive magistrate at another—The election of this officer, as well as of the president of the United States seems to be properly secured; but when we examine the powers of the president, and the forms of the executive, we shall perceive that the general government, in this part, will have a strong tendency to aristocracy, or the government of the few. The executive is, in fact the president and senate in all transactions of any importance; the president is connected with, or tied to the senate; he may always act with the senate, but never can effectually counteract its views: The president can appoint no officer, civil or military, who shall not be agreeable to the senate; and the presumption is, that the will of so important a body will not be very easily controuled, and that it will exercise its powers with great address.

In the judicial department, powers ever kept distinct in well balanced governments, are no less improperly blended in the hands of the same men—in the judges of the supreme court is lodged, the law, the equity and the fact. It is not necessary to pursue the minute organical parts of the general government proposed.—There were various interests in the convention, to be reconciled, especially of large and small states; of carrying and non-carrying states: and of states more and states less democratic—vast labour and attention were by the convention bestowed on the organization of the parts of the constitution offered; still it is acknowledged there are many things radically wrong in the essential parts of this constitution—but it is said that these are the result of our situation: On a full examination of the subject, I believe it; but what do the laborious inquiries and determinations of the convention prove? If they prove any thing, they prove that we cannot consolidate the states on proper principles: The organization of the government presented proves, that we cannot form a general government in which all power can be safely lodged; and a little attention to the parts of the one proposed will make it appear very evident, that all the powers proposed to be lodged in it, will not be then well deposited, either for the purposes of government, or the preservation of liberty. I will suppose no abuse of powers in those cases, in which the abuse of it is not well guarded against—I will suppose the words authorising the general government to regulate the elections of its own members struck out of the plan, or free district elections, in each state, amply secured.—That the small representation provided for shall be as fair and equal as it is capable of being made—I will suppose the judicial department regulated on pure principles, by future laws, as far as it can be by the constitution, and consist with the situation of the country—still there will be an unreasonable accumulation of powers in the general government, if all be granted, enumerated in the plan proposed. The plan does not present a well balanced government. The senatorial branch of the legislative and the executive are substantially united, and the president, or the first executive magistrate, may aid the senatorial interest when weakest, but never can effectually support the democratic, however it may be oppressed;—the excellency, in my mind, of a well balanced government is that it consists of distinct branches, each sufficiently strong and independant to keep its own station, and to aid either of the other branches which may occasionally want aid.

The convention found that any but a small house of representatives would be expensive, and that it would be impracticable to assemble a large number of representatives. Not only the determination of the convention in this case, but the situation of the states, proves the impracticability of collecting, in any one point, a proper representation.

The formation of the senate, and the smallness of the house, being, therefore, the result of our situation, and the actual state of things, the evils which may attend the exercise of many powers in this national government may be considered as without a remedy.

All officers are impeachable before the senate only—before the men by whom they are appointed, or who are consenting to the appointment of these officers. No judgment of conviction, on an impeachment, can be given unless two thirds of the senators agree. Under these circumstances the right of impeachment, in the house, can be of but little importance; the house cannot expect often to convict the offender; and, therefore, probably, will but seldom or never exercise the right. In addition to the insecurity and inconveniences attending this organization beforementioned, it may be observed, that it is extremely difficult to secure the people against the fatal effects of corruption and influence. The power of making any law will be in the president, eight senators, and seventeen representatives, relative to the important objects enumerated in the constitution. Where there is a small representation a sufficient number to carry any measure, may, with ease, be influenced by bribes, offices and civilities; they may easily form private juntoes, and out-door meetings, agree on measures, and carry them by silent votes.

Impressed, as I am, with a sense of the difficulties there are in the way of forming the parts of a federal government on proper principles, and seeing a government so unsubstantially organized, after so arduous an attempt has been made, I am led to believe, that powers ought to be given to it with great care and caution.

In the second place it is necessary, therefore, to examine the extent, and the probable operations of some of those extensive powers proposed to be vested in this government. These powers, legislative, executive and judicial, respect internal as well as external objects. Those respecting external objects, as all foreign concerns, commerce, imposts, all causes arising on the seas, peace and war, and Indian affairs, can be lodged no where else, with any propriety, but in this government. Many powers that respect internal objects ought clearly to be lodged in it; as those to regulate trade between the states, weights and measures, the coin or current monies, post-offices, naturalization, &c. These powers may be exercised without essentially affecting the internal police of the respective states: But powers to lay and collect internal taxes, to form the militia, to make bankrupt laws, and to decide on appeals, questions arising on the internal laws of the respective states, are of a very serious nature, and carry with them almost all other powers. These taken in connection with the others, and powers to raise armies and build navies, proposed to be lodged in this government, appear to me to comprehend all the essential powers in the community, and those which will be left to the states will be of no great importance.

A power to lay and collect taxes at discretion, is, in itself, of very great importance. By means of taxes, the government may command the whole or any part of the subject's property. Taxes may be of various kinds; but there is a strong distinction between external and internal taxes. External taxes are impost duties, which are laid on imported goods; they may usually be collected in a few seaport towns, and of a few individuals, though ultimately paid by the consumer; a few officers can collect them, and they can be carried no higher than trade will bear, or smuggling permit—that in the very nature of commerce, bounds are set to them. But internal taxes, as poll and land taxes, excises, duties on all written instruments, &c. may fix themselves on every person and species of property in the community; they may be carried to any lengths, and in proportion as they are extended, numerous officers must be employed to assess them, and to enforce the collection of them. In the United Netherlands the general government has compleat powers, as to external taxation; but as to internal taxes, it makes requisitions on the provinces. Internal taxation in this country is more important, as the country is so very extensive. As many assessors and collectors of federal taxes will be above three hundred miles from the seat of the federal government as will be less. Besides, to lay and collect internal taxes, in this extensive country, must require a great number of congressional ordinances, immediately operating upon the body of the people; these must continually interfere with the state laws, and thereby produce disorder and general dissatisfaction, till the one system of laws or the other, operating upon the same subjects, shall be abolished. These ordinances alone, to say nothing of those respecting the militia, coin, commerce, federal judiciary, &c. &c. will probably soon defeat the operations of the state laws and governments.

Should the general government think it politic, as some administrations (if not all) probably will, to look for a support in a system of influence, the government will take every occasion to multiply laws, and officers to execute them, considering these as so many necessary props for its own support. Should this system of policy be adopted, taxes more productive than the impost duties will, probably, be wanted to support the government, and to discharge foreign demands, without leaving any thing for the domestic creditors. The internal sources of taxation then must be called into operation, and internal tax laws and federal assessors and collectors spread over this immense country. All these circumstances considered, is it wise, prudent, or safe, to vest the powers of laying and collecting internal taxes in the general government, while imperfectly organized and inadequate; and to trust to amending it hereafter, and making it adequate to this purpose? Is it not only unsafe but absurd to lodge power in a government before it is fitted to receive it? It is confessed that this power and representation ought to go together. Why give the power first? Why give the power to the few, who, when possessed of it, may have address enough to prevent the increase of representation? Why not keep the power, and, when necessary, amend the constitution, and add to its other parts this power, and a proper increase of representation at the same time? Then men who may want the power will be under strong inducements to let in the people, by their representatives, into the government, to hold their due proportion of this power. If a proper representation be impracticable, then we shall see this power resting in the states, where it at present ought to be, and not inconsiderately given up.

When I recollect how lately congress, conventions, legislatures, and people contended in the cause of liberty, and carefully weighed the importance of taxation, I can scarcely believe we are serious in proposing to vest the powers of laying and collecting internal taxes in a government so imperfectly organized for such purposes. Should the United States be taxed by a house of representatives of two hundred members, which would be about fifteen members for Connecticut, twenty-five for Massachusetts, &c. still the middle and lower classes of people could have no great share, in fact, in taxation. I am aware it is said, that the representation proposed by the new constitution is sufficiently numerous; it may be for many purposes; but to suppose that this branch is sufficiently numerous to guard the rights of the people in the administration of the government, in which the purse and sword is placed, seems to argue that we have forgot what the true meaning of representation is. I am sensible also, that it is said that congress will not attempt to lay and collect internal taxes; that it is necessary for them to have the power, though it cannot probably be exercised.—I admit that it is not probable that any prudent congress will attempt to lay and collect internal taxes, especially direct taxes: but this only proves, that the power would be improperly lodged in congress, and that it might be abused by imprudent and designing men.

I have heard several gentlemen, to get rid of objections to this part of the constitution, attempt to construe the powers relative to direct taxes, as those who object to it would have them; as to these, it is said, that congress will only have power to make requisitions, leaving it to the states to lay and collect them. I see but very little colour for this construction, and the attempt only proves that this part of the plan cannot be defended. By this plan there can be no doubt, but that the powers of congress will be complete as to all kinds of taxes whatever—Further, as to internal taxes, the state governments will have concurrent powers with the general government, and both may tax the same objects in the same year; and the objection that the general government may suspend a state tax, as a necessary measure for the promoting the collection of a federal tax, is not without foundation.—As the states owe large debts, and have large demands upon them individually, there clearly would be a propriety in leaving in their possession exclusively, some of the internal sources of taxation, at least until the federal representation shall be properly encreased: The power in the general government to lay and collect internal taxes, will render its powers respecting armies, navies and the militia, the more exceptionable. By the constitution it is proposed that congress shall have power "to raise and support armies, but no appropriation of money to that use shall be for a longer term than two years; to provide and maintain a navy; to provide for calling forth the militia to execute the laws of the union; suppress insurrections, and repel invasions: to provide for organizing, arming, and disciplining the militia": reserving to the states the right to appoint the officers, and to train the militia according to the discipline prescribed by congress; congress will have unlimited power to raise armies, and to engage officers and men for any number of years; but a legislative act applying money for their support can have operation for no longer term than two years, and if a subsequent congress do not within the two years renew the appropriation, or further appropriate monies for the use of the army, the army will be left to take care of itself. When an army shall once be raised for a number of years, it is not probable that it will find much difficulty in getting congress to pass laws for applying monies to its support. I see so many men in America fond of a standing army, and especially among those who probably will have a large share in administering the federal system; it is very evident to me, that we shall have a large standing army as soon as the monies to support them can be possibly found. An army is a very agreeable place of employment for the young gentlemen of many families. A power to raise armies must be lodged some where; still this will not justify the lodging this power in a bare majority of so few men without any checks; or in the government in which the great body of the people, in the nature of things, will be only nominally represented. In the state governments the great body of the people, the yeomanry, &c. of the country, are represented: It is true they will chuse the members of congress, and may now and then chuse a man of their own way of thinking; but it is impossible for forty, or thirty thousand people in this country, one time in ten to find a man who can possess similar feelings, views, and interests with themselves: Powers to lay and collect taxes and to raise armies are of the greatest moment; for carrying them into effect, laws need not be frequently made, and the yeomanry, &c. of the country ought substantially to have a check upon the passing of these laws; this check ought to be placed in the legislatures, or at least in the few men the common people of the country, will, probably, have in congress, in the true sense of the word, "from among themselves". It is true, the yeomanry of the country possess the lands, the weight of property, possess arms, and are too strong a body of men to be openly offended—and, therefore, it is urged, they will take care of themselves, that men who shall govern will not dare pay any disrespect to their opinions. It is easily perceived, that if they have not their proper negative upon passing laws in congress, or on the passage of laws relative to taxes and armies, they may in twenty or thirty years be by means imperceptible to them, totally deprived of that boasted weight and strength: This may be done in a great measure by congress, if disposed to do it, by modelling the militia. Should one fifth or one eighth part of the men capable of bearing arms be made a select militia, as has been proposed, and those the young and ardent part of the community, possessed of but little or no property, and all the others put upon a plan that will render them of no importance, the former will answer all the purposes of an army, while the latter will be defenceless. The state must train the militia in such form and according to such systems and rules as congress shall prescribe: and the only actual influence the respective states will have respecting the militia will be in appointing the officers. I see no provision made for calling out the *posse commitatus* for executing the laws of the union, but provision is made for congress to call forth the militia for the execution of them—and the militia in general, or any select part of it, may be called out under military officers, instead of the sheriff to enforce an execution of federal laws, in the first instance and thereby introduce an entire military execution of the laws. I know that powers to raise taxes, to regulate the military strength of the community on some uniform plan, to provide for its defense and internal order, and for duly executing the laws, must be lodged somewhere; but still we ought not so to lodge them, as evidently to give one order of men in the community, undue advantages over others; or commit the many to the mercy, prudence and moderation of the few. And so far as it may be necessary to lodge any of the peculiar powers in the general government, a more safe exercise of them ought to be secured, by requiring the consent of two-thirds or three-fourths of congress thereto—until the federal representation can be increased, so that the democratic members in congress may stand some tolerable chance of a reasonable negative, in behalf of the numerous, important, and democratic part of the community.

I am not sufficiently acquainted with the laws and internal police of all the states to discern fully, how general bankrupt laws, made by the union, would affect them, or promote the public good. I believe the property of debtors, in the several states, is held responsible for their debts in modes and forms very different. If uniform bankrupt laws can be made without producing real and substantial inconveniences, I wish them to be made by congress.

There are some powers proposed to be lodged in the general government in the judicial department, I think very unnecessarily, I mean powers respecting questions arising upon the internal laws of the respective states. It is proper the federal judiciary should have powers co-extensive with the federal legislature—that is, the power of deciding finally on the laws of the union. By Art. 3. Sect. 2. the powers of the federal judiciary are extended (among other things) to all cases between a state and citizens of another state—between citizens of different states—between a state or the citizens thereof, and foreign states, citizens or subjects. Actions in all these cases, except against a state government, are now brought and finally determined in the law courts of the states respectively; and as there are no words to exclude these courts of their jurisdiction in these cases, they will have concurrent jurisdiction with the inferior federal courts in them; and, therefore, if the new constitution be adopted without any amendment in this respect, all those numerous actions, now brought in the state courts between our citizens and foreigners, between citizens of different states, by state governments against foreigners, and by state governments against citizens of other states, may also be brought in the federal courts; and an appeal will lay in them from the state courts, or federal inferior courts, to the supreme judicial court of the union. In almost all these cases, either party may have the trial by jury in the state courts; excepting paper money and tender laws, which are wisely guarded against in the proposed constitution, justice may be obtained in these courts on reasonable terms; they must be more competent to proper decisions on the laws of their respective states, than the federal courts can possibly be. I do not, in any point of view, see the need of opening a new jurisdiction to these causes—of opening a new scene of expensive law suits—of suffering foreigners, and citizens of different states, to drag each other many hundred miles into the federal courts. It is true, those courts may be so organized by a wise and prudent legislature, as to make the obtaining of justice in them tolerably easy; they may in general be organized on the common law principles of the country: But this benefit is by no means secured by the constitution. The trial by jury is secured only in those few criminal cases, to which the federal laws will extend—as crimes committed on the seas, against the laws of nations, treason, and counterfeiting the federal securities and coin: But even in these cases, the jury trial of the vicinage is not secured—particularly in the large states, a citizen may be tried for a crime committed in the state, and yet tried in some states 500 miles from the place where it was committed; but the jury trial is not secured at all in civil causes. Though the convention have not established this trial, it is to be hoped that congress, in putting the new system into execution, will do it by a legislative act, in all cases in which it can be done with propriety. Whether the jury trial is not excluded [from] the supreme judicial court, is an important question. By Art. 3. Sect. 2. all cases affecting ambassadors, other public ministers, and consuls, and in those cases in which a state shall be party, the supreme court shall have [original] jurisdiction. In all the other cases beforementioned, the supreme court shall have appellate jurisdiction, both as to *law and fact,* with such exception, and under such regulations, as the congress shall make. By court is understood a court consisting of judges; and the idea of a jury is excluded. This court, or the judges, are to have jurisdiction on appeals, in all the cases enumerated, as to law and fact; the judges are to decide the law and try the fact, and the trial of the fact being assigned to the judges by the constitution, a jury for trying the fact is excluded; however, under the exceptions and powers to make regulations, congress may, perhaps, introduce the jury, to try the fact in most necessary cases.

There can be but one supreme court in which the final jurisdiction will centre in all federal causes—except in cases where appeals by law shall not be allowed: The judicial powers of the federal courts extends in law and equity to certain cases: and, therefore, the powers to determine on the law, in equity, and as to the fact, all will concentre in the supreme court:— These powers, which by this constitution are blended in the same hands, the same judges, are in Great-Britain deposited in different hands—to wit, the decision of the law in the law judges, the decision in equity in the chancellor, and the trial of the fact in the jury. It is a very dangerous thing to vest in the same judge power to decide on the law, and also general powers in equity; for if the law restrain him, he is only to step into his shoes of equity, and give what judgment his reason or opinion may dictate; we have no precedents in this country, as yet, to regulate the divisions in equity as in Great-Britain, equity, therefore, in the supreme court for many years will be mere discretion. I confess in the constitution of this supreme court, as left by the constitution, I do not see a spark of freedom or a shadow of our own or the British common law.

This court is to have appellate jurisdiction in all the other cases before mentioned: Many sensible men suppose that cases before mentioned respect, as well the criminal cases as the civil ones, mentioned antecedently in the constitution; if so an appeal is allowed in criminal cases—contrary to the usual sense of law. How far it may be proper to admit a foreigner or the citizen of another state to bring actions against state governments, which have failed in performing so many promises made during the war, is doubtful: How far it may be proper so to humble a state, as to oblige it to answer to an individual in a court of law, is worthy of consideration; the states are now subject to no such actions; and this new jurisdiction will subject the states, and many defendants to actions, and processes, which were not in the contemplation of the parties, when the contract was made; all engagements existing between citizens of different states, citizens and foreigners, states and foreigners; and states and citizens of other states were made the parties contemplating the remedies then existing on the laws of the states—and the new remedy proposed to be given in the federal courts, can be founded on no principle whatever.

Your's, &c.
The FEDERAL FARMER.

Organization and Powers of the
Proposed Government II

DEAR SIR,

IT will not be possible to establish in the federal courts the jury trial of the vicinage so well as in the state courts.

Third. There appears to me to be not only a premature deposit of some important powers in the general government—but many of those deposited there are undefined, and may be used to good or bad purposes as honest or designing men shall prevail. By Art. 1, Sect. 2, representatives and direct taxes shall be apportioned among the several states, &c.—same art. sect. 8, the congress shall have powers to lay and collect taxes, duties, &c. for the common defence and general welfare, but all duties, imposts and excises, shall be uniform throughout the United States. By the first recited clause, direct taxes shall be apportioned on the states. This seems to favour the idea suggested by some sensible men and writers, that congress, as to direct taxes, will only have power to make requisitions; but the latter clause, power to lay and collect taxes, &c. seems clearly to favour the contrary opinion and, in my mind, the true one, that congress shall have power to tax immediately individuals, without the intervention of the state legislatures, in fact the first clause appears to me only to provide that each state shall pay a certain portion of the tax, and the latter to provide that congress shall have power to lay and collect taxes, that is to assess upon, and to collect of the individuals in the state, the state's quota; but these still I consider as undefined powers, because judicious men understand them differently.

It is doubtful whether the vice president is to have any qualifications; none are mentioned; but he may serve as president, and it may be inferred, he ought to be qualified therefore as the president; but the qualifications of the president are required only of the person to be elected president. By art. 2, sect. 2. "But the congress may by law vest the appointment of such inferior officers as they think proper in the president alone, in the courts of law, or in the heads of the departments:" Who are inferior officers? May not a congress disposed to vest the appointment of all officers in the president, under this clause, vest the appointment of almost every officer in the president alone, and destroy the check mentioned in the first part of the clause, and lodged in the senate. It is true, this check is badly lodged, but then some check upon the first magistrate in appointing officers, ought it appears by the opinion of the convention, and by the general opinion, to be established in the constitution.

*The year intended is undoubtedly 1787. Like The Federal Farmer's other letters, this one is on the draft Constitution and actually continues a discussion begun in Letter III.—Ed.

By art. 3, sect. 2, the supreme court shall have appellate jurisdiction as to law and facts with such exceptions, &c. to what extent is it intended the exceptions shall be carried—Congress may carry them so far as to annihilate substantially the appellate jurisdiction, and the clause be rendered of very little importance.

4th. There are certain rights which we have always held sacred in the United States, and recognized in all our constitutions, and which, by the adoption of the new constitution in its present form, will be left unsecured. By article 6, the proposed constitution, and the laws of the United States, which shall be made in pursuance thereof; and all treaties made, or which shall be made under the authority of the United States, shall be the supreme law of the land; and the judges in every state shall be bound thereby; any thing in the constitution or laws of any state to the contrary notwithstanding.

It is to be observed that when the people shall adopt the proposed constitution it will be their last and supreme act; it will be adopted not by the people of New-Hampshire, Massachusetts, &c. but by the people of the United States; and wherever this constitution, or any part of it, shall be incompatible with the ancient customs, rights, the laws or the constitutions heretofore established in the United States, it will entirely abolish them and do them away: And not only this, but the laws of the United States which shall be made in pursuance of the federal constitution will be also supreme laws, and wherever they shall be incompatible with those customs, rights, laws or constitutions heretofore established, they will also entirely abolish them and do them away.

By the article before recited, treaties also made under the authority of the United States, shall be the supreme law: It is not said that these treaties shall be made in pursuance of the constitution—nor are there any constitutional bounds set to those who shall make them: The president and two thirds of the senate will be empowered to make treaties indefinitely, and when these treaties shall be made, they will also abolish all laws and state constitutions incompatible with them. This power in the president and senate is absolute, and the judges will be bound to allow full force to whatever rule, article or thing the president and senate shall establish by treaty, whether it be practicable to set any bounds to those who make treaties, I am not able to say: if not, it proves that this power ought to be more safely lodged.

The federal constitution, the laws of congress made in pursuance of the constitution, and all treaties must have full force and effect in all parts of the United States; and all other laws, rights and constitutions which stand in their way must yield: It is proper the national laws should be supreme, and superior to state or district laws: but then the national laws ought to yield to unalienable or fundamental rights—and national laws, made by a few men, should extend only to a few national objects. This will not be the case with the laws of congress: To have any proper idea of their extent, we must carefully examine the legislative, executive and judicial powers proposed to be lodged in the general government, and consider them in connection with a general clause in art. 1. sect. 8. in these words (after enumerating a number of powers) "To make all laws which shall be necessary and proper for carrying into execution the foregoing powers, and all other powers vested by this constitution in the government of the United States, or in any department or officer thereof."—The powers of this government as has been observed, extend to internal as well as external objects, and to those objects to which all others are subordinate; it is almost impossible to have a just conception of these powers, or of the extent and number of the laws which may be deemed necessary and proper to carry them into effect, till we shall come to exercise those powers and make the laws. In making laws to carry those powers into effect, it is to be expected, that a wise and prudent congress will pay respect to the opinions of a free people, and bottom their laws on those principles which have been considered as essential and fundamental in the British, and in our government: But a congress of a different character will not be bound by the constitution to pay respect to those principles.

It is said, that when the people make a constitution, and delegate powers, that all powers not delegated by them to those who govern, is reserved in the people; and that the people, in the present case, have reserved in themselves, and in their state governments, every right and power not expressly given by the federal constitution to those who shall administer the national government. It is said, on the other hand, that the people, when they make a constitution, yield all power not expressly reserved to themselves. The truth is, in either case, it is mere matter of opinion, and men usually take either side of the argument, as will best answer their purposes: But the general presumption being, that men who govern, will, in doubtful cases, construe laws and constitutions most favourably for encreasing their own powers; all wise and prudent people, in forming constitutions, have drawn the line, and carefully described the powers parted with and the powers reserved. By the state constitutions, certain rights have been reserved in the people; or rather, they have been recognized and established in such a manner, that state legislatures are bound to respect them, and to make no laws infringing upon them. The state legislatures are obliged to take notice of the bills of rights of their respective states. The bills of rights, and the state constitutions, are fundamental compacts only between those who govern, and the people of the same state.

In the year 1788 the people of the United States make a federal constitution, which is a fundamental compact between them and their federal rulers; these rulers, in the nature of things, cannot be bound to take notice of any other compact. It would be absurd for them, in making laws, to look over thirteen, fifteen, or twenty state constitutions, to see what rights are established as fundamental, and must not be infringed upon, in making laws in the society. It is true, they would be bound to do it if the people, in their federal compact, should refer to the state constitutions, recognize all parts not inconsistent with the federal constitution, and direct their federal rulers to take notice of them accordingly; but this is not the case, as the plan stands proposed at present; and it is absurd, to suppose so unnatural an idea is intended or implied. I think my opinion is not only founded in reason, but I think it is supported by the report of the convention itself. If there are a number of rights established by the state constitutions, and which will remain sacred, and the general government is bound to take notice of them—it must take notice of one as well as another; and if unnecessary to recognize or establish one by the federal constitution, it would be unnecessary to recognize or establish another by it. If the federal constitution is to be construed so far in connection with the state constitutions, as to leave the trial by jury in civil causes, for instance, secured; on the same principles it would have left the trial by jury in criminal causes, the benefits of the writ of habeas corpus, &c. secured; they all stand on the same footing; they are the common rights of Americans, and have been recognized by the state constitutions: But the convention found it necessary to recognize or re-establish the benefits of that writ, and the jury trial in criminal cases. As to *ex post facto* laws, the convention has done the same in one case, and gone further in another. It is a part of the compact between the people of each state and their rulers, that no *ex post facto* laws shall be made. But the convention, by Art. 1. Sect. 10 have put a sanction upon this part even of the state compacts. In fact, the 9th and 10th Sections in Art. 1. in the proposed constitution, are no more nor less, than a partial bill of rights; they establish certain principles as part of the compact upon which the federal legislators and officers can never infringe. It is here wisely stipulated, that the federal legislature shall never pass a bill of attainder, or *ex post facto* law; that no tax shall be laid on articles exported, &c. The establishing of one right implies the necessity of establishing another and similar one.

On the whole, the position appears to me to be undeniable, that this bill of rights ought to be carried farther, and some other principles established, as a part of this fundamental compact between the people of the United States and their federal rulers.

It is true, we are not disposed to differ much, at present, about religion; but when we are making a constitution, it is to be hoped, for ages and millions yet unborn, why not establish the free exercise of religion, as a part of the national compact. There are other essential rights, which we have justly understood to be the rights of freemen; as freedom from hasty and unreasonable search warrants, warrants not founded on oath, and not issued with due caution, for searching and seizing men's papers, property, and persons. The trials by jury in civil causes, it is said, varies so much in the several states, that no words could be found for the uniform establishment of it. If so, the federal legislation will not be able to establish it by any general laws. I confess I am of opinion it may be established, but not in that beneficial manner in which we may enjoy it, for the reasons beforementioned. When I speak of the jury trial of the vicinage, or the trial of the fact in the neighbourhood,—I do not lay so much stress upon the circumstance of our being tried by our neighbours: in this enlightened country men may be probably impartially tried by those who do not live very near them: but the trial of facts in the neighbourhood is of great importance in other respects. Nothing can be more essential than the cross examining witnesses, and generally before the triers of the facts in question. The common people can establish facts with much more ease with oral than written evidence; when trials of facts are removed to a distance from the homes of the parties and witnesses, oral evidence becomes intolerably expensive, and the parties must depend on written evidence, which to the common people is expensive and almost useless; it must be frequently taken ex porte, and but very seldom leads to the proper discovery of truth.

The trial by jury is very important in another point of view. It is essential in every free country, that common people should have a part and share of influence, in the judicial as well as in the legislative department. To hold open to them the offices of senators, judges, and offices to fill which an expensive education is required, cannot answer any valuable purposes for them; they are not in a situation to be brought forward and to fill those offices; these, and most other offices of any considerable importance, will be occupied by the few. The few, the well born, &c. as Mr. Adams calls them, in judicial decisions as well as in legislation, are generally disposed, and very naturally too, to favour those of their own description.

The trial by jury in the judicial department, and the collection of the people by their representatives in the legislature, are those fortunate inventions which have procured for them, in this country, their true proportion of influence, and the wisest and most fit means of protecting themselves in the community. Their situation, as jurors and representatives, enables them to acquire information and knowledge in the affairs and government of the society; and to come forward, in turn, as the centinels and guardians of each other. I am very sorry that even a few of our countrymen should consider jurors and representatives in a different point of view, as ignorant troublesome bodies, which ought not to have any share in the concerns of government.

I confess I do not see in what cases the congress can, with any pretence of right, make a law to suppress the freedom of the press; though I am not clear, that congress is restrained from laying any duties whatever on printing, and from laying duties particularly heavy on certain pieces printed, and perhaps congress may require large bonds for the payment of these duties. Should the printer say, the freedom of the press was secured by the constitution of the state in which he lived, congress might, and perhaps, with great propriety, answer, that the federal constitution is the only compact existing between them and the people; in this compact the people have named no others, and therefore congress, in exercising the powers assigned them, and in making laws to carry them into execution, are restrained by nothing beside the federal constitution, any more than a state legislature is restrained by a compact between the magistrates and people of a county, city, or town of which the people, in forming the state constitution, have taken no notice.

It is not my object to enumerate rights of inconsiderable importance; but there are others, no doubt, which ought to be established as a fundamental part of the national system.

It is worthy [of] observation, that all treaties are made by foreign nations with a confederacy of thirteen states—that the western country is attached to thirteen states—thirteen states have jointly and severally engaged to pay the public debts.—Should a new government be formed of nine, ten, eleven, or twelve states, those treaties could not be considered as binding on the foreign nations who made them. However, I believe the probability to be, that if nine states adopt the constitution, the others will.

It may also be worthy [of] our examination, how far the provision for amending this plan, when it shall be adopted, is of any importance. No measures can be taken towards amendments, unless two-thirds of the congress, or two-thirds of the legislatures of the several states shall agree.— While power is in the hands of the people, or democratic part of the community, more especially as at present, it is easy, according to the general course of human affairs, for the few influential men in the community, to obtain conventions, alterations in government, and to persuade the common people they may change for the better, and to get from them a part of the power: But when power is once transferred from the many to the few, all changes become extremely difficult; the government, in this case, being beneficial to the few, they will be exceedingly artful and adroit in preventing any measures which may lead to a change; and nothing will produce it, but great exertions and severe struggles on the part of the common people. Every man of reflection must see that the change now proposed, is a transfer of power from the many to the few, and the probability is, the artful and ever active aristocracy, will prevent all peaceable measures for changes, unless when they shall discover some favourable moment to increase their own influence. I am sensible, thousands of men in the United States, are disposed to adopt the proposed constitution, though they perceive it to be essentially defective, under an idea that amendments of it, may be obtained when necessary. This is a pernicious idea, it argues a servility of character totally unfit for the support of free government; it is very repugnant to that perpetual jealousy respecting liberty, so absolutely necessary in all free states, spoken of by Mr. Dickinson.—However, if our countrymen are so soon changed, and the language of 1774, is become odious to them, it will be in vain to use the language of freedom, or to attempt to rouse them to free enquiries: But I shall never believe this is the case with them, whatever present appearances may be, till I shall have very strong evidence indeed of it.

Your's, &c.
The FEDERAL FARMER

V

The Struggle over Ratification
of the Constitution I

DEAR SIR,

THUS I have examined the federal constitution as far as a few days leisure would permit. It opens to my mind a new scene; instead of seeing powers cautiously lodged in the hands of numerous legislators, and many magistrates, we see all important powers collecting in one centre, where a few men will possess them almost at discretion. And instead of checks in the formation of the government, to secure the rights of the people against the usurpations of those they appoint to govern, we are to understand the equal division of lands among our people, and the strong arm furnished them by nature and situation, are to secure them against those usurpations. If there are advantages in the equal division of our lands, and the strong and manly habits of our people, we ought to establish governments calculated to give duration to them, and not governments which never can work naturally, till that equality of property, and those free and manly habits shall be destroyed; these evidently are not the natural basis of the proposed constitution. No man of reflection, and skilled in the science of government, can suppose these will move on harmoniously together for ages, or even for fifty years. As to the little circumstances commented upon, by some writers, with applause—as the age of a representative, of the president, &c.—they have, in my mind, no weight in the general tendency of the system.

There are, however, in my opinion, many good things in the proposed system. It is founded on elective principles, and the deposits of powers in different hands, is essentially right. The guards against those evils we have experienced in some states in legislation are valuable indeed; but the value of every feature in this system is vastly lessened for the want of that one important feature in a free government, a representation of the people. Because we have sometimes abused democracy, I am not among those men who think a democratic branch a nuisance; which branch shall be sufficiently numerous, to admit some of the best informed men of each order in the community into the administration of government.

While the radical defects in the proposed system are not so soon discovered, some temptations to each state, and to many classes of men to adopt it, are very visible. It uses the democratic language of several of the state constitutions, particularly that of Massachusetts; the eastern states will receive advantages so far as the regulation of trade, by a bare majority, is committed to it: Connecticut and New-Jersey will receive their share of a general impost: The middle states will receive the advantages surrounding the seat of government: The southern states will receive protection, and have their negroes represented in the legislature, and large back countries will soon have a majority in it. This system promises a large field of employment to military gentlemen, and gentlemen of the law; and in case the government shall be executed without convulsions, it will afford security to creditors, to the clergy, salary-men and others depending on money payments. So far as the system promises justice and reasonable advantages, in these respects, it ought to be supported by all honest men; but whenever it promises unequal and improper advantages to any particular states, or orders of men, it ought to be opposed.

I have, in the course of these letters observed, that there are many good things in the proposed constitution, and I have endeavoured to point out many important defects in it. I have admitted that we want a federal system—that we have a system presented, which, with several alterations may be made a tolerable good one—I have admitted there is a well founded uneasiness among creditors and mercantile men. In this situation of things, you ask me what I think ought to be done? My opinion in this case is only the opinion of an individual, and so far only as it corresponds with the opinions of the honest and substantial part of the community, is it entitled to consideration. Though I am fully satisfied that the state conventions ought most seriously to direct their exertions to altering and amending the system proposed before they shall adopt it—yet I have not sufficiently examined the subject, or formed an opinion, how far it will be practicable for those conventions to carry their amendments. As to the idea, that it will be in vain for those conventions to attempt amendments, it cannot be admitted; it is impossible to say whether they can or not until the attempt shall be made; and when it shall be determined, by experience, that the conventions cannot agree in amendments, it will then be an important question before the people of the United States, whether they will adopt or not the system proposed in its present form. This subject of consolidating the states is new; and because forty or fifty men have agreed in a system, to suppose the good sense of this country, an enlightened nation, must adopt it without examination, and though in a state of profound peace, without endeavouring to amend those parts they perceive are defective, dangerous to freedom, and destructive of the valuable principles of republican government—is truly humiliating. It is true there may be danger in delay, but there is danger in adopting the system in its present form, and I see the danger in either case will arise principally from the conduct and views of two very unprincipled parties in the United States—two fires, between which the honest and substantial people have long found themselves situated. One party is composed of little insurgents, men in debt, who want no law, and who want a share of the property of others; these are called levellers, Shayites,* &c. The other party is composed

*It is reasonable to assume that this is intended as a reference to participants in the Shays' Rebellion of 1786 and their sympathizers. For details relating to this rebellion, see Robert J. Taylor, *Western Massachusetts in the Revolution* (Providence, Rhode Island: Brown University Press, 1954), Chaps. VI and VII.—Ed.

of a few, but more dangerous men, with their servile dependents; these avariciously grasp at all power and property; you may discover in all the actions of these men, an evident dislike to free and equal government, and they will go systematically to work to change, essentially, the forms of government in this country; these are called aristocrats, m—ites, &c. &c. Between these two parties is the weight of the community; the men of middling property, men not in debt on the one hand, and men, on the other, content with republican governments, and not aiming at immense fortunes, offices, and power. In 1786, the little insurgents, the levellers, came forth, invaded the rights of others, and attempted to establish governments according to their wills. Their movements evidently gave encouragement to the other party, which, in 1787, has taken the political field, and with its fashionable dependants, and the tongue and the pen, is endeavouring to establish in great haste, a politer kind of government. These two parties, which will probably be opposed or united as it may suit their interests and views, are really insignificant compared with the solid, free, and independent part of the community. It is not my intention to suggest, that either of these parties, and the real friends of the proposed consitution, are the same men. The fact is, these aristocrats support and hasten the adoption of the proposed constitution, merely because they think it is a stepping stone to their favorite object. I think I am well founded in this idea; I think the general politics of these men support it, as well as the common observation among them, That the proffered plan is the best that can be got at present, it will do for a few years, and lead to something better. The sensible and judicious part of the community will carefully weigh all these circumstances; they will view the late convention as a respectable assembly of men—America probably never will see an assembly of men, of a like number, more respectable. But the members of the convention met without knowing the sentiments of one man in ten thousand in these states respecting the new ground taken. Their doings are but the first attempts in the most important scene ever opened. Though each individual in the state conventions will not, probably, be so respectable as each individual in the federal convention, yet as the state conventions will probably consist of fifteen hundred or two thousand men of abilities, and versed in the science of government, collected from all parts of the community and from all orders of men, it must be acknowledged that the weight of respectability will be in them—In them will be collected the solid sense and the real political character of the country. Being revisers of the subject, they will possess peculiar advantages. To say that these conventions ought not to attempt, coolly and deliberately, the revision of the system, or that they cannot amend it, is very foolish or very assuming. If these conventions, after examining the system, adopt it, I shall be perfectly satisfied, and wish to see men make the administration of the government an equal blessing to all orders of men. I believe the great body of our people to be virtuous and friendly to good government, to the protection of liberty and property; and it is the duty of all good men, especially of those who are placed as centinels to guard their rights—it is their duty to examine into the prevailing politics of parties, and to disclose them—while they avoid exciting undue suspicions, to lay facts before the people, which will enable them to form a proper judgment. Men who wish the people of this country to determine for themselves, and deliberately to fit the government to their situation, must feel some degree of indignation at those attempts to hurry the adoption of a system, and to shut the door against examination. The very attempts create suspicions, that those who make them have secret views, or see some defects in the system, which, in the hurry of affairs, they expect will escape the eye of a free people.

What can be the views of those gentlemen in Pennsylvania, who precipitated decisions on this subject? What can be the views of those gentlemen in Boston, who countenanced the Printers in shutting up the press against a fair and free investigation of this important system in the usual way. The members of the convention have done their duty—why should some of them fly to their states—almost forget a propriety of behaviour, and precipitate measures for the adoption of a system of their own making? I confess candidly, when I consider these circumstances in connection with the unguarded parts of the system I have mentioned, I feel disposed to proceed with very great caution, and to pay more attention than usual to the conduct of particular characters. If the constitution presented be a good one, it will stand the test with a well informed people: all are agreed there shall be state conventions to examine it; and we must believe it will be adopted, unless we suppose it is a bad one, or that those conventions will make false divisions respecting it. I admit improper measures are taken against the adoption of the system as well for it—all who object to the plan proposed ought to point out the defects objected to, and to propose those amendments with which they can accept it, or to propose some other system of government, that the public mind may be known, and that we may be brought to agree in some system of government, to strengthen and execute the present, or to provide a substitute. I consider the field of enquiry just opened, and that we are to look to the state conventions for ultimate decisions on the subject before us; it is not to be presumed, that they will differ about small amendments, and lose a system when they shall have made it substantially good; but touching the essential amendments, it is to be presumed the several conventions will pursue the most rational measures to agree in and obtain them; and such defects as they shall discover and not remove, they will probably notice, keep them in view as the ground work of future amendments, and in the firm and manly language which every free people ought to use, will suggest to those who may hereafter administer the government, that it is their expectation, that the system will be so organized by legislative acts, and the government so administered, as to render those defects as little injurious as possible. Our countrymen are entitled to an honest and faithful government; to a government of laws and not of men; and also to one of their chusing—as a citizen of the country, I wish to see these objects secured, and licentious, assuming, and overbearing men restrained; if the constitution or social compact be vague and unguarded, then we depend wholly upon the prudence, wisdom and moderation of those who manage the affairs of government; or on what, probably, is equally uncertain and precarious, the success of the people oppressed by the abuse of government, in receiving it from the hands of those who abuse it, and placing it in the hands of those who will use it well.

In every point of view, therefore, in which I have been able, as yet, to contemplate this subject, I can discern but one rational mode of proceeding relative to it: and that is to examine it with freedom and candour, to have state conventions some months hence, which shall examine coolly every article, clause, and word in the system proposed, and to adopt it with such amendments as they shall think fit. How far the state conventions ought to pursue the mode prescribed by the federal convention of adopting or rejecting the plan in toto, I leave it to them to determine. Our examination of the subject hitherto has been rather of a general nature. The republican characters in the several states, who wish to make this plan more adequate to security of liberty and property, and to the duration of the principles of a free government, will, no doubt, collect their opinions to certain points, and accurately define those alterations and amendments they wish; if it shall be found they essentially disagree in them, the conventions will then be able to determine whether to adopt the plan as it is, or what will be proper to be done.

Under these impressions, and keeping in view the improper and unadvisable lodgment of powers in the general government, organized as it at present is, touching internal taxes, armies and militia, the elections of its own members, causes between citizens of different states, &c. and the want of a more perfect bill of rights, &c. I drop the subject for the present, and when I shall have leisure to revise and correct my ideas respecting it, and to collect into points the opinions of those who wish to make the system more secure and safe, perhaps I may proceed to point out particularly for your consideration, the amendments which ought to be ingrafted into this system, not only in conformity to my own, but the deliberate opinions of others—you will with me perceive, that the objections to the plan proposed may, by a more leisure examination be set in a stronger point of view, especially the important one, that there is no substantial representation of the people provided for in a government in which the most essential powers, even as to the internal police of the country, is proposed to be lodged.

I think the honest and substantial part of the community will wish to see this system altered, permanency and consistency given to the constitution we shall adopt; and therefore they will be anxious to apportion the powers to the features and organization of the government, and to see abuse in the exercise of power more effectually guarded against. It is suggested, that state officers, from interested motives will oppose the constitution presented—I see no reason for this, their places in general will not be affected, but new openings to offices and places of profit must evidently be made by the adoption of the constitution in its present form.

Your's, &c.
The FEDERAL FARMER.

To the REPUBLICAN.

THE
FEDERAL FARMER'S
SECOND PAMPHLET

AN ADDITIONAL NUMBER

OF

LETTERS

PROM THE

FEDERAL FARMER

TO THE

REPUBLICAN;

LEADING TO A FAIR EXAMINATION

OF THE

SYSTEM OF GOVERNMENT,

PROPOSED BY THE LATE

CONVENTION;

TO SEVERAL ESSENTIAL AND NECES-
SARY ALTERATIONS IN IT;

And calculated to Illustrate and Support the

PRINCIPLES AND POSITIONS

Laid down in the preceding

LETTERS.

TITLE PAGE OF THE FEDERAL FARMER'S
SECOND PAMPHLET, CONTAINING LETTERS VI–XVIII
(COURTESY OF THE LIBRARY OF CONGRESS)

VI

The Struggle over Ratification
of the Constitution II

DEAR SIR,

MY former letters to you, respecting the constitution proposed, were calculated merely to lead to a fuller investigation of the subject; having more extensively considered it, and the opinions of others relative to it, I shall, in a few letters, more particularly endeavour to point out the defects, and propose amendments. I shall in this make only a few general and introductory observations, which, in the present state of the momentous question, may not be improper; and I leave you, in all cases, to decide by a careful examination of my works, upon the weight of my arguments, the propriety of my remarks, the uprightness of my intentions, and the extent of my candor—I presume I am writing to a man of candor and reflection, and not to an ardent, peevish, or impatient man.

When the constitution was first published, there appeared to prevail a misguided zeal to prevent a fair unbiassed examination of a subject of infinite importance to this people and their posterity—to the cause of liberty and the rights of mankind—and it was the duty of those who saw a restless ardor, or design, attempting to mislead the people by a parade of names and misrepresentations, to endeavour to prevent their having their intended effects. The only way to stop the passions of men in their career is, coolly to state facts, and deliberately to avow the truth—and to do this we are frequently forced into a painful view of men and measures.

Since I wrote to you in October, I have heard much said, and seen many pieces written, upon the subject in question; and on carefully examining them on both sides, I find much less reason for changing my sentiments, respecting the good and defective parts of the system proposed than I expected—The opposers, as well as the advocates of it, confirm me in my opinion, that this system affords, all circumstances considered, a better basis to build upon than the confederation. And as to the principal defects, as the smallness of the representation, the insecurity of elections, the undue mixture of powers in the senate, the insecurity of some essential rights, &c. the opposition appears, generally, to agree respecting them, and many of the ablest advocates virtually to admit them—Clear it is, the latter do not attempt manfully to defend these defective parts, but to cover them with a mysterious veil; they concede, they retract; they say we could do no better; and some of them, when a little out of temper, and hard pushed, use arguments that do more honor to their ingenuity, than to their candor and firmness.

Three states have now adopted the constitution without amendments; these, and other circumstances, ought to have their weight in deciding the question, whether we will put the system into operation, adopt it, enumerate and recommend the necessary amendments, which afterwards, by three-fourths of the states, may be ingrafted into the system, or whether we will make the amendments prior to the adoption—I only undertake to shew amendments are essential and necessary—how far it is practicable to ingraft them into the plan, prior to the adoption, the state conventions must determine. Our situation is critical, and we have but our choice of evils—We may hazard much by adopting the constitution in its present form—we may hazard more by rejecting it wholly—we may hazard much by long contending about amendments prior to the adoption. The greatest political evils that can befall us, are discords and civil wars—the greatest blessings we can wish for, are peace, union, and industry, under a mild, free, and steady government. Amendments recommended will tend to guard and direct the administration—but there will be danger that the people, after the system shall be adopted, will become inattentive to amendments—Their attention is now awake—the discussion of the subject, which has already taken place, has had a happy effect—it has called forth the able advocates of liberty, and tends to renew, in the minds of the people, their true republican jealousy and vigilance, the strongest guard against the abuses of power; but the vigilance of the people is not sufficiently constant to be depended on—Fortunate it is for the body of a people, if they can continue attentive to their liberties, long enough to erect for them a temple, and constitutional barriers for their permanent security: when they are well fixed between the powers of the rulers and the rights of the people, they become visible boundaries, constantly seen by all, and any transgression of them is immediately discovered: they serve as centinels for the people at all times, and especially in those unavoidable intervals of inattention.

Some of the advocates, I believe, will agree to recommend *good* amendments; but some of them will only consent to recommend indefinite, specious, but unimportant ones; and this only with a view to keep the door open for obtaining, in some favourable moment, their main object, a complete consolidation of the states, and a government much higher toned, less republican and free than the one proposed. If necessity, therefore, should ever oblige us to adopt the system, and recommend amendments, the true friends of a federal republic must see they are well defined, and well calculated, not only to prevent our system of government moving further from republican principles and equality, but to bring it back nearer to them—they must be constantly on their guard against the address, flattery, and man-oeuvres of their adversaries.

The gentlemen who oppose the constitution, or contend for amendments in it, are frequently, and with much bitterness, charged with wantonly attacking the men who framed it. The unjustness of this charge leads me to make one observation upon the conduct of parties, &c. Some of the advocates are only pretended federalists; in fact they wish for an abolition of the state governments. Some of them I believe to be honest federalists, who wish to preserve *substantially* the state governments united under an efficient federal head; and many of them are blind tools without any object. Some of the opposers also are only pretended federalists, who want no federal government, or one merely advisory. Some of them are the true federalists, their object, perhaps, more clearly seen, is the same with that of the honest federalists; and some of them, probably, have no distinct object. We might as well call the advocates and opposers tories and whigs, or any thing else, as federalists and anti-federalists. To be for or against the constitution, as it stands, is not much evidence of a federal disposition; if any names are applicable to the parties, on account of their general politics, they are those of republicans and anti-republicans. The opposers are generally men who support the rights of the body of the people, and are properly republicans. The advocates are generally men not very friendly to those rights, and properly anti-republicans.

Had the advocates left the constitution, as they ought to have done, to be adopted or rejected on account of its own merits or imperfections, I do not believe the gentlemen who framed it would ever have been even alluded to in the contest by the opposers. Instead of this, the ardent advocates begun by quoting names as incontestible authorities for the implicit adoption of the system, without any examination—treated all who opposed it as friends of anarchy; and with an indecent virulence addressed M—n G—y, L—e,* and almost every man of weight they could find in the opposition by name. If they had been candid men they would have applauded the moderation of the opposers for not retaliating in this pointed manner, when so fair an opportunity was given them; but the opposers generally saw that it was no time to heat the passions; but, at the same time, they saw there was something more than mere zeal in many of their adversaries; they saw them attempting to mislead the people, and to precipitate their divisions, by the sound of names, and forced to do it, the opposers, in general terms, alledged those names were not of sufficient authority to justify the hasty adoption of the system contended for. The convention, as a body, was undoubtedly respectable; it was, gener-

---

*The reference here is probably to George Mason, Elbridge Gerry, and Richard Henry Lee, all of whom participated in efforts to prevent ratification of the Constitution in the form in which it came from the Federal Convention of 1787.—Ed.

ally, composed of members of the then and preceding Congresses: as a body of respectable men we ought to view it. To select individual names, is an invitation to personal attacks, and the advocates, for their own sake, ought to have known the abilities, politics, and situation of some of their favourite characters better, before they held them up to view in the manner they did, as men entitled to our implicit political belief: they ought to have known, whether all the men they so held up to view could, for their past conduct in public offices, be approved or not by the public records, and the honest part of the community. These ardent advocates seem now to be peevish and angry, because, by their own folly, they have led to an investigation of facts and of political characters, unfavourable to them, which they had not the discernment to foresee. They may well apprehend they have opened a door to some Junius, or to some man, after his manner, with his polite addresses to men by name, to state serious facts, and unfold the truth; but these advocates may rest assured, that cool men in the opposition, best acquainted with the affairs of the country, will not, in the critical passage of a people from one constitution to another, pursue inquiries, which, in other circumstances, will be deserving of the highest praise. I will say nothing further about political characters, but examine the constitution; and as a necessary and previous measure to a particular examination, I shall state a few general positions and principles, which receive a general assent, and briefly notice the leading features of the confederation, and several state conventions, to which, through the whole investigation, we must frequently have recourse, to aid the mind in its determinations.

We can put but little dependance on the partial and vague information transmitted to us respecting antient governments; our situation as a people is peculiar: our people in general have a high sense of freedom; they are high spirited, though capable of deliberate measures; they are intelligent, discerning, and well informed; and it is to their condition we must mould the constitution and laws. We have no royal or noble families, and all things concur in favour of a government entirely elective. We have tried our abilities as freemen in a most arduous contest, and have succeeded; but we now find the main springs of our movements were the love of liberty, and a temporary ardor, and not any energetic principle in the federal system.

Our territories are far too extensive for a limited monarchy, in which the representatives must frequently assemble, and the laws operate mildly and systematically. The most eligible system is a federal republic, that is, a system in which national concerns may be transacted in the centre, and local affairs in state or district governments.

The powers of the union ought to be extended to commerce, the coin, and national objects; and a division of powers, and a deposit of them in different hands, is safest.

Good government is generally the result of experience and gradual improvements, and a punctual execution of the laws is essential to the preservation of life, liberty, and property. Taxes are always necessary, and the power to raise them can never be safely lodged without checks and limitation, but in a full and substantial representation of the body of the people; the quantity of power delegated ought to be compensated by the brevity of the time of holding it, in order to prevent the possessors increasing it. The supreme power is in the people, and rulers possess only that portion which is expressly given them; yet the wisest people have often declared this is the case on proper occasions, and have carefully formed stipulations to fix the extent, and limit the exercise of the power given.

The people by Magna Charta, &c. did not acquire powers, or receive privileges from the king, they only ascertained and fixed those they were entitled to as Englishmen; the title used by the king "we grant," was mere form. Representation, and the jury trial, are the best features of a free government ever as yet discovered, and the only means by which the body of the people can have their proper influence in the affairs of government.

In a federal system we must not only balance the parts of the same government, as that of the state, or that of the union; but we must find a balancing influence between the general and local governments—the latter is what men or writers have but very little or imperfectly considered.

A free and mild government is that in which no laws can be made without the formal and free consent of the people, or of their constitutional representatives; that is, of a substantial representative branch. Liberty, in its genuine sense, is security to enjoy the effects of our honest industry and labours, in a free and mild government, and personal security from all illegal restraints.

Of rights, some are natural and unalienable, of which even the people cannot deprive individuals: Some are constitutional or fundamental; these cannot be altered or abolished by the ordinary laws; but the people, by express acts, may alter or abolish them—These, such as the trial by jury, the benefits of the writ of habeas corpus, &c. individuals claim under the solemn compacts of the people, as constitutions, or at least under laws so strengthened by long usage as not to be repealable by the ordinary legislature—and some are common or mere legal rights, that is, such as individuals claim under laws which the ordinary legislature may alter or abolish at pleasure.

The confederation is a league of friendship among the states or sovereignties for the common defence and mutual welfare—Each state expressly retains its sovereignty, and all powers not expressly given to congress—All federal powers are lodged in a congress of delegates annually elected by the state legislatures, except in Connecticut and Rhode-Island, where they are chosen by the people—Each state has a vote in congress, pays its delegates, and may instruct or recall them; no delegate can hold any office of profit, or serve more than three years in any six years—Each state may be represented by not less than two, or more than seven delegates.

Congress (nine states agreeing) may make peace and war, treaties and alliances, grant letters of marque and reprisal, coin money, regulate the alloy and value of the coin, require men and monies of the states by fixed proportions, and appropriate monies, form armies and navies, emit bills of credit, and borrow monies.

Congress (seven states agreeing) may send and receive ambassadors, regulate captures, make rules for governing the army and navy, institute courts for the trial of piracies and felonies committed on the high seas, and for settling territorial disputes between the individual states, regulate weight and measures, post-offices, and Indian affairs.

No state, without the consent of congress, can send or receive embassies, make any agreement with any other state, or a foreign state, keep up any vessels of war or bodies of forces in time of peace, or engage in war, or lay any duties which may interfere with the treaties of congress—Each state must appoint regimental officers, and keep up a well regulated militia—Each state may prohibit the importation or exportation of any species of goods.

The free inhabitants of one state are entitled to the privileges and immunities of the free citizens of the other states—Credit in each state shall be given to the records and judicial proceedings in the others.

Canada, acceding, may be admitted, and any other colony may be admitted by the consent of nine states.

Alterations may be made by the agreement of congress, and confirmation of all the state legislatures.

The following, I think, will be allowed to be unalienable or fundamental rights in the United States:—

No man, demeaning himself peaceably, shall be molested on account of his religion or mode of worship—The people have a right to hold and enjoy their property according to known standing laws, and which cannot be taken from them without their consent, or the consent of their representatives; and whenever taken in the pressing urgencies of government, they are to receive a reasonable compensation for it—Individual security consists in having free recourse to the laws—The people are subject to no laws or taxes not assented to by their representatives constitutionally assembled—They are at all times entitled to the benefits of the writ of habeas corpus, the trial by jury in criminal and civil causes—They have a right when charged to a speedy trial in the vicinage; to be heard by themselves or counsel, not to be compelled to furnish evidence against themselves, to have witnesses face to face, and to confront their adversaries before the judge—No man is held to answer a crime charged upon him till it be substantially described to him; and he is subject to no unreasonable searches or seizures of his person, papers or effects—The people have a right to assemble in an orderly manner, and petition the government for a redress of wrongs—The freedom of the press ought not to be restrained—No emoluments, except for actual service—No hereditary honors, or orders of nobility, ought to be allowed—The military ought to be subordinate to the civil authority, and no soldier be quartered on the citizens without their consent—The militia ought always to be armed and disciplined, and the usual defence of the country—The supreme power is in the people, and power delegated ought to return to them at stated periods, and frequently—The legislative, executive, and judicial powers, ought always to be kept distinct—others perhaps might be added.

The organization of the state governments—Each state has a legislature, an executive, and a judicial branch—In general legislators are excluded from the important executive and judicial offices—Except in the Carolinas there is no constitutional distinction among Christian sects—The constitutions of New-York, Delaware, and Virginia, exclude the clergy from offices civil and military—the other states do nearly the same in practice.

Each state has a democratic branch elected twice a year in Rhode-Island and Connecticut, biennially in South-Carolina, and annually in the other states—There are about 1500 representatives in all the states, or one to each 1700 inhabitants, reckoning five blacks for three whites—The states do not differ as to the age or moral characters of the electors or elected, nor materially as to their property.

Pennsylvania has lodged all her legislative powers in a single branch, and Georgia has done the same; the other eleven states have each in their legislatures a second or senatorial branch. In forming this they have combined various principles, and aimed at several checks and balances. It is amazing to see how ingenuity has worked in the several states to fix a barrier against popular instability. In Massachusetts the senators are apportioned on districts according to the taxes they pay, nearly according to property. In Connecticut the freemen, in September, vote for twenty counsellers, and return the names of those voted for in the several towns; the legislature takes the twenty who have the most votes, and gives them to the people, who, in April, chuse twelve of them, who, with the governor and deputy governor, form the senatorial branch. In Maryland the senators are chosen by two electors from each county; these electors are chosen by the freemen, and qualified as the members in the democratic branch are: In these two cases checks are aimed at in the mode of election. Several states have taken into view the periods of service, age, property, &c. In South-Carolina a senator is elected for two years, in Delaware three, and in New-York and Virginia four, in Maryland five, and in the other states for one. In New-York and Virginia one-fourth part go out yearly. In Virginia a senator must be twenty-five years old, in South-Carolina thirty. In New-York the electors must each have a freehold worth 250 dollars, in North-Carolina a freehold of fifty acres of land; in the other states the electors of senators are qualified as electors of representatives are. In Massachusetts a senator must have a freehold in his own right worth 1000 dollars, or any estate worth 2000, in New-Jersey any estate worth 2666, in South-Carolina worth 1300 dollars, in North-Carolina

300 acres of land in fee, &c. The numbers of senators in each state are from ten to thirty-one, about 160 in the eleven states, about one to 14000 inhabitants.

Two states, Massachusetts and New-York, have each introduced into their legislatures a third, but incomplete branch. In the former, the governor may negative any law not supported by two-thirds of the senators, and two-thirds of the representatives: in the latter, the governor, chancellor, and judges of the supreme court may do the same.

Each state has a single executive branch. In the five eastern states the people at large elect their governors; in the other states the legislatures elect them. In South-Carolina the governor is elected once in two years; in New-York and Delaware once in three, and in the other states annually. The governor of New-York has no executive council, the other governors have. In several states the governor has a vote in the senatorial branch—the governors have similar powers in some instances, and quite dissimilar ones in others. The number of executive counsellers in the states are from five to twelve. In the four eastern states, New-Jersey, Pennsylvania, and Georgia, they are of the men returned legislators by the people. In Pennsylvania the counsellers are chosen triennially, in Delaware every fourth year, in Virginia every three years, in South-Carolina biennially, and in the other states yearly.

Each state has a judicial branch; each common law courts, superior and inferior; some chancery and admiralty courts: The courts in general sit in different places, in order to accommodate the citizens. The trial by jury is had in all the common law courts, and in some of the admiralty courts. The democratic freemen principally form the juries; men destitute of property, of character, or under age, are excluded as in elections. Some of the judges are during good behavior, and some appointed for a year, and some for years and all are dependant on the legislatures for their salaries—Particulars respecting this department are too many to be noticed here.

The FEDERAL FARMER.

VII

The Ratio of Representatives
to Constituents I

DECEMBER 31, 1787.

DEAR SIR,

IN viewing the various governments instituted by mankind, we see their whole force reducible to two principles—the important springs which alone move the machines, and give them their intended influence and controul, are force and persuasion: by the former men are compelled, by the latter they are drawn. We denominate a government despotic or free, as the one or other principle prevails in it. Perhaps it is not possible for a government to be so despotic, as not to operate persuasively on some of its subjects; nor is it, in the nature of things, I conceive, for a government to be so free, or so supported by voluntary consent, as never to want force to compel obedience to the laws. In despotic governments one man, or a few men, independant of the people, generally make the laws, command obedience, and enforce it by the sword: one fourth part of the people are armed, and obliged to endure the fatigues of soldiers, to oppress the others and keep them subject to the laws. In free governments the people, or their representatives, make the laws; their execution is principally the effect of voluntary consent and aid; the people respect the magistrate, follow their private pursuits, and enjoy the fruits of their labour with very small deductions for the public use. The body of the people must evidently prefer the latter species of government; and it can be only those few, who may be well paid for the part they take in enforcing despotism, that can, for a moment, prefer the former. Our true object is to give full efficacy to one principle, to arm persuasion on every side, and to render force as little necessary as possible. Persuasion is never dangerous not even in despotic governments; but military force, if often applied internally, can never fail to destroy the love and confidence, and break the spirits, of the people; and to render it totally impracticable and unnatural for him or them who govern, and yield to this force against the people, to hold their places by the peoples' elections.

I repeat my observation, that the plan proposed will have a doubtful operation between the two principles; and whether it will preponderate towards persuasion or force is uncertain.

Government must exist—If the persuasive principle be feeble, force is infallibly the next resort—The moment the laws of congress shall be disregarded they must languish, and the whole system be convulsed—that moment we must have recourse to this next resort, and all freedom vanish.

It being impracticable for the people to assemble to make laws, they must elect legislators, and assign men to the different departments of the government. In the representative branch we must expect chiefly to collect the confidence of the people, and in it to find almost entirely the force of persuasion. In forming this branch, therefore, several important considerations must be attended to. It must possess abilities to discern the situation of the people and of public affairs, a disposition to sympathize with the people, and a capacity and inclination to make laws congenial to their circumstances and condition: it must afford security against interested combinations, corruption and influence; it must possess the confidence, and have the voluntary support of the people.

I think these positions will not be controverted, nor the one I formerly advanced, that a fair and equal representation is that in which the interests, feelings, opinions and views of the people are collected, in such manner as they would be were the people all assembled. Having made these general observations, I shall proceed to consider further my principal position, viz. that there is no substantial representation of the people provided for in a government, in which the most essential powers, even as to the internal police of the country, are proposed to be lodged and to propose certain amendments as to the representative branch: 1st. That there ought to be *an increase of the numbers of representatives:* And, 2dly. That the elections of them ought to be better secured.

1. The representation is unsubstantial and ought to be increased. In matters where there is much room for opinion, you will not expect me to establish my positions with mathematical certainty; you must only expect my observations to be candid, and such as are well founded in the mind of the writer. I am in a field where doctors disagree; and as to genuine representation, though no feature in government can be more important, perhaps, no one has been less understood, and no one that has received so imperfect a consideration by political writers. The ephori in Sparta, and the tribunes in Rome, were but the shadow; the representation in Great-Britain is unequal and insecure. In America we have done more in establishing this important branch on its true principles, than, perhaps, all the world besides: yet even here, I conceive, that very great improvements in representation may be made. In fixing this branch, the situation of the people must be surveyed, and the number of representatives and forms of election apportioned to that situation. When we find a numerous people settled in a fertile and extensive country, possessing equality, and few or none of them oppressed with riches or wants, it ought to be the anxious care of the constitution and laws, to arrest them from national depravity, and to preserve them in their happy condition. A virtuous people make just laws, and good laws tend to preserve unchanged a virtuous people. A virtuous and happy people by laws uncongenial to their characters, may easily be gradually changed into servile and depraved creatures. Where the people, or their representatives, make the laws, it is probable they will generally be fitted to the national character and circumstances, unless the representation be partial, and the imperfect substitute of the people. However, the people may be electors, if the representation be so formed as to give one or more of the natural classes of men in the society an undue ascendency over the others, it is imperfect; the former will gradually become masters, and the latter slaves. It is the first of all among the political balances, to preserve in its proper station each of these classes. We talk of balances in the legislature, and among the departments of government; we ought to carry them to the body of the people. Since I advanced the idea of balancing the several orders of men in a community, in forming a genuine representation, and [have] seen that idea considered as chimerical, I have been sensibly struck with a sentence in the marquis Beccaria's treatise: this sentence was quoted by congress in 1774, and is as follows:—"In every society there is an effort continually tending to confer on one part the height

of power and happiness, and to reduce the others to the extreme of weakness and misery; the intent of good laws is to oppose this effort, and to diffuse their influence universally and equally." Add to this Montesquieu's opinion, that "in a free state every man, who is supposed to be a free agent, ought to be concerned in his own government: therefore, the legislative should reside in the whole body of the people, or their representatives." It is extremely clear that these writers had in view the several orders of men in society, which we call aristocratical, democratical, merchantile, mechanic, &c. and perceived the efforts they are constantly, from interested and ambitious views, disposed to make to elevate themselves and oppress others. Each order must have a share in the business of legislation actually and efficiently. It is deceiving a people to tell them they are electors, and can chuse their legislators, if they cannot, in the nature of things, chuse men from among themselves, and genuinely like themselves. I wish you to take another idea along with you; we are not only to balance these natural efforts, but we are also to guard against accidental combinations; combinations founded in the connections of offices and private interests, both evils which are increased in proportion as the number of men, among which the elected must be, are decreased. To set this matter in a proper point of view, we must form some general ideas and descriptions of the different classes of men, as they may be divided by occupations and politically: the first class is the aristocratical. There are three kinds of aristocracy spoken of in this country—the first is a constitutional one, which does not exist in the United States in our common acceptation of the word. Montesquieu, it is true, observes, that where a part of the persons in a society, for want of property, age, or moral character, are excluded any share in the government, the others, who alone are the constitutional electors and elected, form this aristocracy; this, according to him, exists in each of the United States, where a considerable number of persons, as all convicted of crimes, under age, or not possessed of certain property, are excluded any share in the government;—the second is an aristocratic faction, a junto of unprincipled men, often distinguished for their wealth or abilities, who combine together and make their object their private interests and aggrandizement; the existence of this description is merely accidental, but particularly to be guarded against. The third is the natural aristocracy; this term we use to designate a respectable order of men, the line between whom and the natural democracy is in some degree arbitrary; we may place men on one side of this line, which others may place on the other, and in all disputes between the few and the many, a considerable number are wavering and uncertain themselves on which side they are, or ought to be. In my idea of our natural aristocracy in the United States, I include about four or five thousand men; and among these I reckon those who have been placed in the offices of governors, of members of Congress, and state senators generally, in the principal officers of Congress, of the army and militia, the superior judges, the most eminent professional men, &c. and men of large property—the other persons and orders in the community form the natural democracy; this includes in general the yeomanry, the subordinate officers, civil and military, the fishermen, mechanics and traders, many of the merchants and professional men. It is easy to perceive that men of these two classes, the aristocratical, and democratical, with views equally honest have sentiments widely different, especially respecting public and private expences, salaries, taxes, &c. Men of the first class associate more extensively, have a high sense of honor, possess abilities, ambition, and general knowledge; men of the second class are not so much used to combining great objects; they possess less ambition, and a larger share of honesty; their dependence is principally on middling and small estates, industrious pursuits, and hard labour, while that of the former is principally on the emoluments of large estates, and of the chief offices of government. Not only the efforts of these two great parties are to be balanced, but other interests and parties also, which do not always oppress each other merely for want of power, and for fear of the consequences: though they, in fact, mutually depend on each other; yet such are their general views, that the merchants alone would never fail to make laws favourable to themselves and oppressive to the farmers, &c. the farmers alone would act on like principles; the former would tax the land, the latter the trade. The manufacturers are often disposed to contend for monopolies, buyers make every exertion to lower prices, and sellers to raise them; men who live by fees and salaries endeavour to raise them, and the part of the people who pay them, endeavour to lower them; the public creditors to augment the taxes, and the people at large to lessen them. Thus, in every period of society, and in all the transactions of men, we see parties verifying the observation made by the Marquis; and those classes which have not their centinels in the government, in proportion to what they have to gain or lose, must infallibly be ruined.

Efforts among parties are not merely confined to property; they contend for rank and distinctions; all their passions in turn are enlisted in political controversies—Men, elevated in society, are often disgusted with the changeableness of the democracy, and the latter are often agitated with the passions of jealousy and envy: the yeomanry possess a large share of property and strength, are nervous and firm in their opinions and habits—the mechanics of towns are ardent and changeable, honest and credulous, they are inconsiderable for numbers, weight and strength, not always sufficiently stable for the supporting free governments: the fishing interest partakes partly of the strength and stability of the landed, and partly of the changeableness of the mechanic interest. As to merchants and traders, they are our agents in almost all money transactions; give activity to government, and possess a considerable share of influence in it. It has been observed by an able writer, that frugal industrious merchants are generally advocates for liberty. It is an observation, I believe, well founded, that the schools produce but few advocates for republican forms of government; gentlemen of the law, divinity, physic, &c. probably form about a fourth part of the people; yet their political influence, perhaps, is equal to that of all the other descriptions of men; if we may judge from the appointments to Congress, the legal characters will often, in a small representation, be the majority; but the more the representatives are encreased, the more of the farmers, merchants, etc. will be found to be brought into the government.

These general observations will enable you to discern what I intend by different classes, and the general scope of my ideas, when I contend for uniting and balancing their interests, feelings, opinions, and views in the legislature; we may not only so unite and balance these as to prevent a change in the government by the gradual exaltation of one part to the depression of others, but we may derive many other advantages from the combination and full representation; a small representation can never be well informed as to the circumstances of the people, the members of it must be too far removed from the people, in general, to sympathize with them, and too few to communicate with them: a representation must be extremely imperfect where the representatives are not circumstanced to make the proper communications to their constituents, and where the constituents in turn cannot, with tolerable convenience, make known their wants, circumstances, and opinions, to their representatives; where there is but one representative to 30,000 or 40,000 inhabitants, it appears to me, he can only mix, and be acquainted with a few respectable characters among his constituents, even double the federal representation, and then there must be a very great distance between the representatives and the people in general represented. On the proposed plan, the state of Delaware, the city of Philadelphia, the state of Rhode-Island, the province of Main, the county of Suffolk in Massachusetts, will have one representative each; there can be but little personal knowledge, or but few communications, between him and the people at large of either of those districts. It has been observed, that mixing only with the respectable men, he will get the best information and ideas from them; he will also receive impressions favourable to their purposes particularly. Many plausible shifts have been made to divert the mind from dwelling on this defective representation, these I shall consider in another place.

Could we get over all our difficulties respecting a balance of interests and party efforts, to raise some and oppress others, the want of sympathy, information and intercourse between the representatives and the people, an insuperable difficulty will still remain, I mean the constant liability of a small number of representatives to private combinations; the tyranny of the one, or the licentiousness of the multitude, are, in my mind, but small evils, compared with the factions of the few. It is a consideration well worth pursuing, how far this house of representatives will be liable to be formed into private juntos, how far influenced by expectations of appointments and offices, how far liable to be managed by the president and senate, and how far the people will have confidence in them. To obviate difficulties on this head, as well as objections to the representative branch, generally, several observations have been made—these I will now examine, and if they shall appear to be unfounded, the objections must stand unanswered.

That the people are the electors, must elect good men, and attend to the administration.

It is said that the members of Congress, at stated periods, must return home, and that they must be subject to the laws they may make, and to a share of the burdens they may impose.

That the people possess the strong arm to overawe their rulers, and the best checks in their national character against the abuses of power, that the supreme power will remain in them.

That the state governments will form a part of, and a balance in the system.

That Congress will have only a few national objects to attend to, and the state governments many and local ones.

That the new Congress will be more numerous than the present, and that any numerous body is unwieldy and mobbish.

That the states only are represented in the present Congress, and that the people will require a representation in the new one; that in fifty or an hundred years the representation will be numerous.

That congress will have no temptation to do wrong; and that no system to enslave the people is practicable.

That as long as the people are free they will preserve free governments; and that when they shall become tired of freedom, arbitrary government must take place.

These observations I shall examine in the course of my letters; and, I think, not only shew that they are not well founded, but point out the fallacy of some of them; and shew, that others do not very well comport with the dignified and manly sentiments of a free and enlightened people.

The FEDERAL FARMER.

VIII

The Ratio of Representatives
to Constituents II

JANUARY 3, 1788.

DEAR SIR,

BEFORE I proceed to examine the objections, I beg leave to add a valuable idea respecting representation, to be collected from De Lome, and other able writers, which essentially tends to confirm my positions: They very justly impute the establishment of general and equal liberty in England to a balance of interests and powers among the different orders of men; aided by a series of fortunate events, that never before [did] and possibly never again will happen.

Before the Norman conquest the people of England enjoyed much of this liberty. The first of the Norman kings, aided by foreign mercenaries and foreign attendants, obnoxious to the English, immediately laid arbitrary taxes, and established arbitrary courts, and severely oppressed all orders of people: The barons and people, who recollected their former liberties, were induced, by those oppressions, to unite their efforts in their common defence: Here it became necessary for the great men, instead of deceiving and depressing the people, to enlighten and court them; the royal power was too strongly fixed to be annihilated, and rational means were, therefore directed to limiting it within proper bounds. In this long and arduous task, in this new species of contests, the barons and people succeeded, because they had been freemen, and knew the value of the object they were contending for; because they were the people of a small island—one people who found it practicable to meet and deliberate in one assembly, and act under one system of resolves, and who were not obliged to meet in different provincial assemblies, as is the case in large countries, as was the case in France, Spain, &c. where their determinations were inconsistent with each other, and where the king could play off one assembly against another.

It was in this united situation the people of England were for several centuries, enabled to combine their exertions, and by compacts, as Magna Charta, a bill of rights, &c. were able to limit, by degrees, the royal prerogatives, and establish their own liberties. The first combination was, probably, the accidental effect of pre-existing circumstances; but there was an admirable balance of interests in it, which has been the parent of English liberty, and excellent regulations enjoyed since that time. The executive power having been uniformly in the king and he the visible head of the nation, it was chimerical for the greatest lord or most popular leader, consistent with the state of the government, and opinion of the people, to seriously think of becoming the king's rival, or to aim at even a share of the executive power, the greatest subject's prospect was only in acquiring a respectable influence in the house of commons, house of lords, or in the ministry; circumstances at once made it the interests of the leaders of the people to stand by them. Far otherwise was it with the ephori in Sparta, and tribunes in Rome. The leaders in England have led the people to freedom, in almost all other countries to servitude. The people in England have made use of deliberate exertions, their safest and most efficient weapons. In other countries they have often acted like mobs, and been enslaved by their enemies, or by their own leaders. In England, the people have been led uniformly, and systematically by their representatives to secure their rights by compact, and to abolish innovations upon the government: they successively obtained Magna Charta, the powers of taxation, the power to propose laws, the habeas corpus act, bill of rights, &c. they, in short, secured general and equal liberty, security to their persons and property; and, as an everlasting security and bulwark of their liberties, they fixed the democratic branch in the legislature, and jury trial in the execution of the laws, the freedom of the press, &c.

In Rome, and most other countries, the reverse of all this is true. In Greece, Rome, and wherever the civil law has been adopted, torture has been admitted. In Rome the people were subject to arbitrary confiscations, and even their lives would be arbitrarily disposed of by consuls, tribunes, dictators, masters, &c. half of the inhabitants were slaves, and the other half never knew what equal liberty was; yet in England the people have had kings, lords, and commons; in Rome they had consuls, senators and tribunes: why then was the government of England so mild and favourable to the body of the people, and that of Rome an ambitious and oppressive aristocracy? Why in England have the revolutions always ended in stipulations in favour of general liberty, equal laws, and the common rights of the people, and in most other countries in favor only of a few influential men? The reasons, in my mind, are obvious: In England the people have been substantially represented in many respects; in the other countries it has not been so. Perhaps a small degree of attention to a few simple facts will illustrate this.—In England, from the oppressions of the Norman kings to the revolution in 1688, during which period of two or three hundred years, the English liberties were ascertained and established, the aristocratic part of that nation was substantially represented by a very large number of nobles, possessing similar interests and feelings with those they represented. The body of the people, about four or five millions, then mostly a frugal landed people, were represented by about five hundred representatives, taken not from the order of men which formed the aristocracy, but from the body of the people, and possessed of the same interests and feelings. De Lome, speaking of the British representation, expressly founds all his reasons on this union; this similitude of interests, feelings, views and circumstances. He observes, the English have preserved their liberties, because they and their leaders or representatives have been strictly united in interests, and in contending for general liberty. Here we see a genuine balance founded in the actual state of things. The whole community, probably, not more than two-fifths more numerous than we now are, were represented by seven or eight hundred men; the barons stipulated with the common people, and the king with the whole. Had the legal distinction between lords and commons been broken down, and the people of that island been called upon to elect forty-five senators, and one hundred and twenty representatives, about the proportion we propose to establish, their whole legislature evidently would have been of the natural aristocracy, and the body of the people would not have had scarcely a single sincere advocate; their interests would have been neglected, general and equal liberty forgot, and the balance lost; contests and conciliations, as in most other countries, would have been merely among the few, and as it might have been necessary to serve their purposes, the people at large would have been flattered or threatened, and probably not a single stipulation made in their favour.

In Rome the people were miserable, though they had three orders, the consuls, senators and tribunes, and approved the laws, and all for want of a genuine representation. The people were too numerous to assemble, and do any thing properly themselves; the voice of a few, the dupes of artifice, was called the voice of the people. It is difficult for the people to defend themselves against the arts and intrigues of the great, but by selecting a suitable number of men fixed to their interest to represent them, and to oppose ministers and senators. And the people's all depends on the number of the men selected, and the manner of doing it. To be convinced of this, we need only attend to the reason of the case, the conduct of the British commons, and of the Roman tribunes: equal liberty prevails in England, because there was a representation of the people, in fact and reality, to establish it; equal liberty never prevailed in Rome, because there was but the shadow of a representation. There were consuls in Rome annually elected to execute the laws, several hundred senators represented the great families; the body of the people annually chose tribunes from among themselves to defend them and to secure their rights; I think the number of tribunes annually chosen never exceeded ten. This representation, perhaps, was not proportionally so numerous as the representation proposed in the new plan; but the difference will not appear to be so great, when it shall be recollected, that these tribunes were chosen annually; that the great patrician families were not admitted to these offices of tribunes, and that the people of Italy who elected the tribunes were a long while, if not always, a small people compared with the people of the United States. What was the consequence of this triffling representation? The people of Rome always elected for their tribunes men conspicuous for their riches, military commands, professional popularity, &c. great commoners, between whom and the noble families there was only the shadowy difference of legal distinction. Among all the tribunes the people chose for several centuries, they had scarcely five real friends to their interests. These tribunes lived, felt and saw, not like the people, but like the great patrician families, like senators and great officers of state, to get into which it was evident by their conduct, was their sole object. These tribunes often talked about the rights and prerogatives of the people, and that was all; for they never even attempted to establish equal liberty: so far from establishing the rights of the people, they suffered the senate, to the exclusion of the people, to engross the powers of taxation; those excellent and almost only real weapons of defence even the people of England possess. The tribunes obtained that the people should be eligible to some of the great offices of state, and marry, if they pleased, into the noble families; these were advantages in their nature, confined to a few elevated commoners, and of triffling importance to the people at large. Nearly the same observations may be made as to the ephori of Sparta.

We may amuse ourselves with names; but the fact is, men will be governed by the motives and temptations that surround their situation. Political evils to be guarded against are in the human character, and not in the name of patrician or plebian. Had the people of Italy, in the early period of the republic, selected yearly, or biennially, four or five hundred of their best informed men, emphatically from among themselves, these representatives would have formed an honest respectable assembly, capable of combining in them the views and exertions of the people, and their respectability would have procured them honest and able leaders, and we should have seen equal liberty established. True liberty stands in need of a fostering hand; from the days of Adam she has found but one temple to dwell in securely; she has laid the foundation of one, perhaps her last, in America; whether this is to be compleated and have duration, is yet a question. Equal liberty never yet found many advocates among the great: it is a disagreeable truth, that power perverts men's views in a greater degree, than public employments inform their understandings—they become hardened in certain maxims, and more lost to fellow feelings. Men may always be too cautious to commit alarming and glaring iniquities; but they, as well as systems, are liable to be corrupted by slow degrees. Junius well observes, we are not only to guard against what men will do, but even against what they may do. Men in high public offices are in stations where they gradually lose sight of the people, and do not often think of attending to them, except when necessary to answer private purposes.

The body of the people must have this true representative security placed somewhere in the nation; and in the United States, or in any extended empire, I am fully persuaded can be placed nowhere, but in the forms of a federal republic, where we can divide and place it in several state or district legislatures, giving the people in these the means of opposing heavy internal taxes and oppressive measures in the proper stages. A great empire contains the amities and animosities of a world within itself. We are not like the people of England, one people compactly settled on a small island, with a great city filled with frugal merchants, serving as a common centre of liberty and union: we are dispersed, and it is impracticable for any but the few to assemble in one place: the few must be watched, checked, and often resisted—tyranny has ever shewn a prediliction to be in close amity with them, or the one man. Drive it from kings and it flies to senators, to decemvirs, to dictators, to tribunes, to popular leaders, to military chiefs, &c.

De Lome well observes, that in societies, laws which were to be equal to all are soon warped to the private interests of the administrators, and made to defend the usurpations of a few. The English, who had tasted the sweets of equal laws, were aware of this, and though they restored their king, they carefully delegated to parliament the advocates of freedom.

I have often lately heard it observed, that it will do very well for a people to make a constitution, and ordain, that at stated periods they will chuse, in a certain manner, a first magistrate, a given number of senators and representatives, and let them have all power to do as they please. This doctrine, however it may do for a small republic, as Connecticut, for instance, where the people may chuse so many senators and representatives to assemble in the legislature, in an eminent degree, the interests, the views, feelings, and genuine sentiments of the people themselves, can never be admitted in an extensive country; and when this power is lodged in the hands of a few, not to limit the few, is but one step short of giving absolute power to one man—in a numerous representation the abuse of power is a common injury, and has no temptation—among the few, the abuse of power may often operate to the private emolument of those who abuse it.

The FEDERAL FARMER.

IX

The Ratio of Representatives
to Constituents III

JANUARY 4, 1788.

DEAR SIR,

THE advocates of the constitution say we must trust to the administration, and elect good men for representatives. I admit, that in forming the social compact, we can fix only general principles, and, of necessity, must trust something to the wisdom and integrity of the administration. But the question is, do we not trust too much, and to men also placed in the vortex of temptation, to lay hold of proffered advantages for themselves and their connections, and to oppress the body of the people.

It is one thing to authorise a well organized legislature to make laws, under the restraints of a well guarded constitution, and another to assemble a few men, and to tell them to do what they please. I am not the more shaken in my principles, or disposed to despair of the cause of liberty, because some of our able men have adopted the yielding language of non-resistance, and writers dare insult the people with the signatures of Caesar, Mark Antony, and of other tyrants; because I see even moderate and amiable men, forced to let go of monarchy in 1775, still in love with it, to use the simile of our countrymen, when the political pot boils, the skum will often get uppermost and make its appearance. I believe the people of America, when they shall fully understand any political subject brought before them, will talk in a very different stile, and use the manly language of freedom.

But "the people must elect good men:"—Examine the system, Is it practicable for them to elect fit and proper representatives where the number is so small? "But the people may chuse whom they please." This is an observation,

I believe, made without due attention to facts and the state of the community. To explain my meaning, I will consider the descriptions of men commonly presented to the people as candidates for the offices of representatives—we may rank them in three classes: 1. The men who form the natural aristocracy, as before defined. 2. Popular demagogues: these men also are often politically elevated, so as to be seen by the people through the extent of large districts; they often have some abilities, without principle, and rise into notice by their noise and arts. 3. The substantial and respectable part of the democracy; they are a numerous and valuable set of men, who discern and judge well, but from being generally silent in public assemblies are often overlooked; they are the most substantial and best informed men in the several towns, who occasionally fill the middle grades of offices, &c. who hold not a splendid, but a respectable rank in private concerns: these men are extensively diffused through all the counties, towns and small districts in the union; even they, and their immediate connections, are raised above the majority of the people, and as representatives are only brought to a level with a more numerous part of the community, the middle orders, and a degree nearer the mass of the people. Hence it is that the best practical representation, even in a small state, must be several degrees more aristocratical than the body of the people. A representation so formed as to admit but few or none of the third class, is, in my opinion, not deserving of the name—even in armies, courts-martial are so formed as to admit subaltern officers into them. The true idea is, so to open and enlarge the representation as to let in a due proportion of the third class with those of the first. Now, my opinion is, that the representation proposed is so small as that ordinarily very few or none of them can be elected; and, therefore, after all the parade of words and forms, the government must possess the soul of aristocracy, or something worse, the spirit of popular leaders.

I observed in a former letter, that the state of Delaware, of Rhode-Island, the Province of Main, and each of the great counties in Massachusetts, &c. would have one member, and rather more than one when the representatives shall be increased to one for each 30,000 inhabitants. In some districts the people are more dispersed and unequal than in others: In Delaware they are compact, in the Province of Main dispersed; how can the elections in either of those districts be regulated so as that a man of the third class can be elected?—Exactly the same principles and motives, the same uncontroulable circumstances, must govern the elections as in the choice of the governors. Call upon the people of either of those districts to chuse a governor, and it will, probably, never happen that they will not bestow a major part, or the greatest number, of their votes on some very conspicuous or very popular character. A man that is known among a few thousand of people, may be quite unknown among thirty or forty thousand. On the whole, it appears to me to be almost a self-evident position, that when we call on thirty or forty thousand inhabitants to unite in giving their votes for one man it will be uniformly impracticable for them to unite in any men, except those few who have become eminent for their civil or military rank, or their popular legal abilities: it will be found totally impracticable for men in the private walks of life, except in the profession of the law, to become conspicuous enough to attract the notice of so many electors and have their suffrages.

But if I am right, it is asked why so many respectable men advocate the adoption of the proposed system. Several reasons may be given—many of our gentlemen are attached to the principles of monarchy and aristocracy; they have an aversion to democratic republics. The body of the people have acquired large powers and substantial influence by the revolution. In the unsettled state of things, their numerous representatives, in some instances, misused their powers and have induced many good men suddenly to adopt ideas unfavourable to such republics, and which ideas they will discard on reflection. Without scrutinizing into the particulars of the proposed system, we immediately perceive that its general tendency is to collect the powers of government, now in the body of the people in reality, and to place them in the higher orders and fewer hands; no wonder then that all those of and about these orders are attached to it; they feel there is something in this system advantageous to them. On the other hand, the body of the people evidently feel there is something wrong and disadvantageous to them; both descriptions perceive there is something tending to bestow on the former the height of power and happiness, and to reduce the latter to weakness, insignificance, and misery. The people evidently feel all this though they want expressions to convey their ideas. Further, even the respectable part of the democracy, have never yet been able to distinguish clearly where the fallacy lies; they find there are defects in the confederation; they see a system presented, they think something must be done, and, while their minds are in suspense the zealous advocates force a reluctant consent. Nothing can be a stronger evidence of the nature of this system, than the general sense of the several orders in the community respecting its tendency; the parts taken generally by them proves my position, that notwithstanding the parade of words and forms, the government must possess the soul of aristocracy.

Congress, heretofore, have asked for moderate additional powers, the cry was give them—be federal but the proper distinction between the cases that produce this disposition, and the system proposed, has not been fairly made and seen in all its consequences. We have seen some of our state representations too numerous, and without examining a medium we run into the opposite extreme. It is true, the proper number of federal representatives is matter of opinion in some degree; but there are extremes which we immediately perceive, and others which we clearly discover on examination. We should readily pronounce a representative branch of 15 members small in a federal government, having complete powers as to taxes, military matters, commerce, the coin &c. &c. On the other hand, we should readily pronounce a federal representation as numerous as those of the several states, consisting of about 1500 representatives, unwieldly and totally improper. It is asked, has not the wisdom of the convention found the medium? Perhaps not: The convention was divided on this point of numbers; at least some of its ablest members urged, that instead of 65 representatives there ought to be 130 in the first instance: They fixed one representative for each 40,000 inhabitants, and at the close of the work, the president suggested, that the representation appeared to be too small and without debate, it was put at, not exceeding one for each 30,000. I mention these facts to shew, that the convention went on no fixed data. In this extensive country it is difficult to get a representation sufficiently numerous: Necessity, I believe, will oblige us to sacrifice in some degree the true genuine principles of representation: But this sacrifice ought to be as little as possible: How far we ought to increase the representation I will not pretend to say; but that we ought to increase it very considerably, is clear—to double it at least, making full allowances for the state representations: and this we may evidently do and approach accordingly toward safety and perfection without encountering any inconveniences. It is with great difficulty the people can unite these different interests and views even tolerably, in the state senators, who are more than twice as numerous as the federal representatives, as proposed by the convention; even these senators are considered as so far removed from the people, that they are not allowed immediately to hold their purse strings.

The principal objections made to the increase of the representation are, the expence and difficulty in getting the members to attend. The first cannot be important; the last, if founded, is against any federal government. As to the expence, I presume, the house of representatives will not be in session more than four months in the year. We find by experience, that about two-thirds of the members of representative assemblies usually attend; therefore, of the representation proposed by the convention, about forty-five members probably will attend, doubling their number, about 90 will probably attend: their pay, in one case, at four dollars a day each (which is putting it high enough) will amount to, yearly, 21,600 dollars; in the other case, 43,200 dollars difference 21,600 dollars;—reduce the state representatives from 1500 down to 1000, and thereby save the attendance of two-thirds of the 500, say three months in a year at one dollar and a quarter a day each, 37,125 dollars. Thus we may leave the state representations sufficient large, and yet save enough by the reduction nearly to support exceeding well the whole federal representation I propose. Surely we never can be so unwise as to sacrifice, essentially, the all-important principles of representation for so small a sum as 21,000 dollars a year for the United States; a single company of soldiers would cost this sum. It is a fact that can easily be shewn that we expend three times this sum every year upon useless inferior offices and very triffling concerns. It is also a fact which can be shewn, that the United States in the late war suffered more by a faction in the federal government, than the pay of the federal representation will amount to for twenty years.

As to the attendance—Can we be so unwise as to establish an unsafe and inadequate representative branch, and give it as a reason, that we believe only a few members will be induced to attend; we ought certainly to establish an adequate representative branch, and adopt measures to induce an attendance; I believe that a due proportion of 130 or 140 members may be induced to attend: there are various reasons for the non-attendance of the members of the present congress; it is to be presumed that these will not exist under the new system.

To compensate for the want of a genuine representation in a government, where the purse and sword, and all important powers, are proposed to be lodged, a variety of unimportant things are enumerated by the advocates of it.

In the second place, it is said the members of congress must return home, and share in the burdens they may impose; and, therefore, private motives will induce them to make mild laws, to support liberty, and ease the burdens of the people: this brings us to a mere question of interest under this head. I think these observations will appear, on examination, altogether fallacious; because this individual interest, which may coincide with the rights and interests of the people, will be far more than balanced by opposite motives and opposite interests. If, on a fair calculation, a man will gain more by measures oppressive to others than he will lose by them, he is interested in their adoption. It is true, that those who govern, generally, by increasing the public burdens increase their own share of them: but by this increase they may, and often do, increase their salaries, fees, and emoluments, in a ten-fold proportion, by increasing salaries, forming armies and navies, and by making offices—If it shall appear the members of congress will have these temptations before them, the argument is on my side—they will view the account, and be induced continually to make efforts advantageous to themselves and connections, and oppressive to others.

We must examine facts—Congress, in its present form, have but few offices to dispose of worth the attention of the members, or of men of the aristocracy; yet, from 1774 to this time, we find a large proportion of those offices assigned to those who were or had been members of congress, and though the states chuse annually sixty or seventy members, many of them have been provided for: but few men are known to congress in this extensive country, and, probably, but few will be to the president and senate, except those who have or shall appear as members of congress, or those whom the members may bring forward. The states may now chuse yearly ninety-one members of congress; under the new constitution they will have it in their power to chuse exactly the same number, perhaps afterwards, one hundred and fifteen, but these must be chosen once in two and six years; so that, in the course of ten years together, not more than two-thirds so many members of congress will be elected and brought into view, as there now are under the confederation in the same term of time: but at least there will be five, if not ten times, as many offices and places worthy the attention of the members, under the new constitution, as there are under the confederation: therefore, we may fairly presume, that a very great proportion of the members of congress, especially the influential ones, instead of returning to private life, will be provided for with lucrative offices, in the civil or military department, and not only the members, but many of their sons, friends, and connection. These offices will be in the constitutional disposition of the president and senate, and, corruption out of the question, what kind of security can we expect in a representation, so many of the members of which may rationally feel themselves candidates for these offices?—let common sense decide. It is true, that members chosen to offices must leave their seats in congress, and to some few offices they cannot be elected till the time shall be expired for which they were elected members; but this scarcely will effect the biass arising from the hopes and expectations of office.

It is not only in this point of view, the members of congress, by their efforts, may make themselves and friends powerful and happy, while the people may be oppressed: but there is another way in which they may soon warp laws, which ought to be equal, to their own advantages, by those imperceptible means, and on those doubtful principles which may not alarm. No society can do without taxes; they are the efficient means of safety and defence, and they too have often been the weapons by which the blessings of society have been destroyed. Congress will have power to lay taxes at pleasure for the general welfare; and if they mis-judge of the general welfare, and lay unnecessary oppressive taxes, the constitution will provide, as I shall hereafter shew, no remedy for the people or states—the people must bear them, or have recourse, not to any constitutional checks or remedies, but to that resistence which is the last resort, and founded in self-defence.

It is well stipulated, that all duties, imposts, and excises shall be equal; and that direct taxes shall be apportioned on the several states by a fixed rule, but nothing further. Here commences a dangerous power in matters of taxation, lodged without any regard to the balance of interests of the different orders of men, and without any regard to the internal policy of the states. Congress having assigned to any state its quota, say to New-Jersey, 80,000 dollars in a given tax, congress will be entirely at liberty to apportion that sum on the counties and towns, polls, lands, houses, labour, &c. and appoint the assessors and collectors in that state in what manner they please; there will be nothing to prevent a system of tax laws being made, unduly to ease some descriptions of men and burden others: though such a system may be unjust and injudicious, though we may complain, the answer will be, congress have the power delegated by the people, and, probably, congress has done what it thought best.

By the confederation taxes must be quotaed on the several states by fixed rules, as before mentioned: but then each state's quota is apportioned on the several numbers and classes of citizens in the state by the state legislature, assessed and collected by state laws. Great pains have been taken to confound the two cases, which are as distinct as light and darkness; this I shall endeavour to illustrate, when I come to the amendment respecting internal taxes. I shall only observe, at present, that in the state legislatures the body of the people will be genuinely represented, and in congress not; that the right of resisting oppressive measures is inherent in the people, and that a constitutional barrier should be so formed, that their genuine representatives may stop an oppressive ruinous measure in its early progress, before it shall come to maturity, and the evils of it become in a degree fixed.

It has lately been often observed, that the power or body of men intrusted with the national defence and tranquility, must necessarily possess the purse unlimitedly, that the purse and sword must go together—this is new doctrine in a free country, and by no means tenable. In the British government the king is particularly intrusted with the national honor and defence, but the commons solely hold the purse. I think I have amply shewn that the representation in congress will be totally inadequate in matters of taxation, &c. and, therefore, that the ultimate controul over the purse must be lodged elsewhere.

We are not to expect even honest men rigidly to adhere to the line of strict impartiality, where the interest of themselves or friends is particularly concerned; if we do expect it, we shall deceive ourselves, and make a wrong estimate of human nature.

But it is asked how shall we remedy the evil, so as to complete and perpetuate the temple of equal laws and equal liberty? Perhaps we never can do it. Possibly we never may be able to do it in this immense country, under any one system of laws however modified; nevertheless, at present, I think the experiment worth a making. I feel an aversion to the disunion of the states, and to separate confederacies; the states have fought and bled in a common cause, and great dangers too may attend these confederacies. I think the system proposed capable of very considerable degrees of perfection, if we pursue first principles. I do not think that De Lome, or any writer I have seen, has sufficiently pursued the proper inquiries and efficient means for making representation and balances in government more perfect; it is our task to do this in America. Our object is equal liberty, and equal laws diffusing their influence among all orders of men; to obtain this we must guard against the biass of interest and passions, against interested combinations, secret or open; we must aim at a balance of efforts and strength.

Clear it is, by increasing the representation we lessen the prospects of each member of congress being provided for in public offices; we proportionably lessen official influence, and strengthen his prospects of becoming a private citizen, subject to the common burdens, without the compensation of the emoluments of office. By increasing the representation we make it more difficult to corrupt and influence the members; we diffuse them more extensively among the body of the people, perfect the balance, multiply information, strengthen the confidence of the people, and consequently support the laws on equal and free principles. There are two other ways, I think, of obtaining in some degree the security we want; the one is, by excluding more extensively the members from being appointed to offices; the other is, by limiting some of their powers; but these two I shall examine hereafter.

The FEDERAL FARMER

X

The Ratio of Representatives
to Constituents IV

JANUARY 7, 1788.

DEAR SIR,

IT is said that our people have a high sense of freedom, possess power, property, and the strong arm; meaning, I presume, that the body of the people can take care of themselves, and awe their rulers; and, therefore, particular provision in the constitution for their security may not be essential. When I come to examine these observations, they appear to me too triffling and loose to deserve a serious answer.

To palliate for the smallness of the representation, it is observed, that the state governments in which the people are fully represented, necessarily form a part of the system. This idea ought to be fully examined. We ought to enquire if the convention have made the proper use of these essential parts; the state governments then we are told will stand between the arbitrary exercise of power and the people: true they may, but armless and helpless, perhaps, with the privilege of making a noise when hurt—this is no more than individuals may do. Does the constitution provide a single check for a single measure, by which the state governments can constitutionally and regularly check the arbitrary measures of congress? Congress may raise immediately fifty thousand men, and twenty millions of dollars in taxes, build a navy, model the militia, &c. and all this constitutionally. Congress may arm on every point, and the state governments can do no more than an individual, by petition to congress, suggest their measures are alarming and not right.

I conceive the position to be undeniable, that the federal government will be principally in the hands of the natural aristocracy, and the state governments principally in the hands of the democracy, the representatives of the body of the people. These representatives in Great-Britain hold the purse, and have a negative upon all laws. We must yield to circumstances, and depart something from this plan, and strike out a new medium, so as to give efficacy to the whole system, supply the wants of the union, and leave the several states, or the people assembled in the state legislatures, the means of defence.

It has been often mentioned, that the objects of congress will be few and

national, and require a small representation; that the objects of each state will
be many and local, and require a numerous representation. This circumstance has not the weight of a feather in my mind. It is certainly unadvisable to
lodge in 65 representatives, and 26 senators, unlimited power to establish
systems of taxation, armies, navies, model the militia, and to do everything
that may essentially tend soon to change, totally, the affairs of the community; and to assemble 1500 state representatives, and 160 senators, to make
fence laws, and laws to regulate the descent and conveyance of property, the
administration of justice between man and man, to appoint militia officers,
&c.

It is not merely the quantity of information I contend for. Two taxing
powers may be inconvenient; but the point is, congress, like the senate of
Rome, will have taxing powers, and the people no check—when the power is
abused, the people may complain and grow angry, so may the state governments; they may remonstrate and counteract, by passing laws to prohibit the
collection of congressional taxes; but these will be acts of the people, acts of
sovereign power, the denier resort unknown to the constitution; acts operating in terrorum, acts of resistence, and not the exercise of any constitutional
power to stop or check a measure before matured: a check properly is the
stopping, by one branch in the same legislature, a measure proposed by the
other in it. In fact the constitution provides for the states no check, properly
speaking, upon the measures of congress—Congress can immediately enlist
soldiers, and apply to the pockets of the people.

These few considerations bring us to the very strong distinction between
the plan that operates on federal principles, and the plan that operates on
consolidated principles. A plan may be federal or not as to its organization;
each state may retain its vote or not; the sovereignty of the state may be
represented, or the people of it. A plan may be federal or not as to its
operations—federal when it requires men and monies of the states, and the
states as such make the laws for raising the men and monies—Not federal,
when it leaves the state governments out of the question, and operates
immediately upon the persons and property of the citizens. The first is the
case with the confederation, the second with the new plan: in the first the
state governments may be check, in the last none at all. This distinction I shall
pursue further hereafter, under the head before mentioned, of amendments
as to internal taxes. And here I shall pursue a species of checks which writers
have not often noticed.

To excuse the smallness of the representation, it is said the new congress
will be more numerous than the old one. This is not true; and for the facts I
refer you to my letter of the 4th instant, to the plan and confederation;
besides there is no kind of similitude between the two plans. The confederation is a mere league of the states, and congress is formed with the particular
checks, and possess the united powers, enumerated in my letter of the 25th
ult. The new plan is totally a different thing: a national government to many

purposes administered, by men chosen for two, four, and six years, not recallable, and among whom there will be no rotation; operating immediately in all money and military matters, &c. on the persons and property of the citizens—I think, therefore, that no part of the confederation ought to be adduced for supporting or injuring the new constitution. It is also said that the constitution gives no more power to congress than the confederation, respecting money and military matters; that congress, under the confederation, may require men and monies to any amount, and the states are bound to comply. This is generally true; but, I think, I shall in a subsequent letter satisfactorily prove, that the states have well founded checks for securing their liberties.

I admit the force of the observation, that all the federal powers, by the confederation, are lodged in a single assembly; however, I think much more may be said in defence of the leading principles of the confederation. I do not object to the qualifications of the electors of representatives, and I fully agree that the people ought to elect one branch.

Further, it may be observed, that the present congress is principally an executive body, which ought not to be numerous; that the house of representatives will be a mere legislative branch, and being the democratic one, ought to be numerous. It is one of the greatest advantages of a government of different branches, that each branch may be conveniently made conformable to the nature of the business assigned it, and all be made conformable to the condition of the several orders of the people. After all the possible checks and limitations we can devise, the powers of the union must be very extensive; the sovereignty of the nation cannot produce the object in view, the defence and tranquility of the whole, without such powers, executive and judicial. I dislike the present congress a single, assembly, because it is impossible to fit it to receive those powers: the executive and judicial powers, in the nature of things, ought to be lodged in a few hands, the legislature in many hands; therefore, want of safety, and unavoidable hasty measures, out of the question, they never can all be lodged in one assembly properly—it, in its very formation, must imply a contradiction.

In objection to increasing the representation, it has also been observed, that it is difficult to assemble a hundred men or more without making them tumultuous and a mere mob; reason and experience do not support this observation. The most respectable assemblies we have any knowledge of and the wisest, have been those, each of which consisted of several hundred members; as the senate of Rome, of Carthage, of Venice, the British Parliament, &c. &c. I think I may without hazarding much, affirm, that our more numerous state assemblies and conventions have universally discovered more wisdom, and as much order, as the less numerous ones: There must be also a very great difference between the characters of two or three hundred men assembled from a single state, and the characters of the number or half the number assembled from all the united states.

It is added, that on the proposed plan the house of representatives in fifty or a hundred years, will consist of several hundred members: The plan will begin with sixty-five, and we have no certainty that the number ever will be encreased, for this plain reason—that all that combination of interests and influence which has produced this plan, and supported so far, will constantly oppose the increase of the representation, knowing that thereby the government will become more free and democratic: But admitting, after a few years, there will be a member for each 30,000 inhabitants, the observation is trifling, the government is in a considerable measure to take its tone from its early movements, and by means of a small representation it may in half of 50 or 100 years, get moved from its basis, or at least so far as to be incapable of ever being recovered. We ought, therefore, on every principle now to fix the government on proper principles, and fit to our present condition—when the representation shall become too numerous, alter it; or we may now make provision, that when the representation shall be increased to a given number, that then there shall be one for each given number of inhabitants, &c.

Another observation is, that congress will have no temptations to do wrong—the men that make it must be very uninformed, or suppose they are talking to children. In the first place, the members will be governed by all those motives which govern the conduct of men, and have before them all the allurements of offices and temptations, to establish unequal burdens, before described. In the second place, they and their friends, probably, will find it for their interests to keep up large armies, navies, salaries, &c. and in laying adequate taxes. In the third place, we have no good grounds to presume, from reason or experience, that it will be agreeable to their characters or views, that the body of the people should continue to have power effectually to interfere in the affairs of government. But it is confidently added, that congress will not have it in their power to oppress or enslave the people, that the people will not bear it. It is not supposed that congress will act the tyrant immediately, and in the face of daylight. It is not supposed congress will adopt important measures, without plausible pretences, especially those which may tend to alarm or produce opposition. We are to consider the natural progress of things: that men unfriendly to republican equality will go systematically to work, gradually to exclude the body of the people from any share in the government, first of the substance, and then of the forms. The men who will have these views will not be without their agents and supporters. When we reflect, that a few years ago we established democratic republics, and fixed the state governments as the barriers between congress and the pockets of the people; what great progress has been made in less than seven years to break down those barriers, and essentially to change the principles of our governments, even by the armless few: is it chimerical to suppose that in fifteen or twenty years to come, that much more can be performed, especially after the adoption of the constitution, when the few will be so much better armed with power and influence, to continue the struggle? Probably, they

will be wise enough never to alarm, but gradually prepare the minds of the
people for one specious change after another, till the final object shall be
obtained. Say the advocates, these are only possibilities—they are prob-
abilities, a wise people ought to guard against; and the address made use of to
keep the evils out of sight, and the means to prevent them, confirm my
opinion.

But to obviate all objections to the proposed plan in the last resort: it is said
our people will be free, so long as they possess the habits of freemen, and
when they lose them, they must receive some other forms of government. To
this I shall only observe, that this is very humiliating language, and can, I
trust, never suit a manly people, who have contended nobly for liberty, and
declared to the world they will be free.

I have dwelt much longer than I expected upon the increasing the representation, the democratic interest in the federal system; but I hope the
importance of the subject will justify my dwelling upon it. I have pursued it in
a manner new, and I have found it necessary to be somewhat prolix, to
illustrate the point I had in view. My idea has ever been, when the democratic
branch is weak and small, the body of the people have no defence, and
everything to fear; if they expect to find genuine political friends in kings and
nobles, in great and powerful men, they deceive themselves. On the other
hand, fix a genuine democratic branch in the government, solely to hold the
purse, and with the power of impeachment, and to propose and negative
laws, cautiously limit the king and nobles, or the executive and the senate, as
the case may be, and the people, I conceive, have but little to fear, and their
liberties will be always secure.

I think we are now arrived to a new era in the affairs of men, when the true
principles of government will be more fully unfolded than heretofore, and a
new world, as it were, grow up in America. In contemplating representation,
the next thing is the security of elections. Before I proceed to this, I beg leave
to observe, that the pay of the representatives of the people is essentially
connected with their interests.

Congress may put the pay of the members unreasonably high, or so low as
that none but the rich and opulent can attend; there are very strong reasons
for supposing the latter, probably, will be the case, and a part of the same
policy, which uniformly and constantly exerts itself to transfer power from
the many to the few. Should the pay be well fixed, and made alterable by
congress, with the consent of a majority of the state legislatures, perhaps, all
the evils to be feared on this head might, in the best practicable manner, be
guarded against, and proper security introduced. It is said the state legislatures fix their own pay—the answer is, that congress is not, nor can it ever be
well formed on those equal principles the state legislatures are. I shall not
dwell on this point, but conclude this letter with one general observation,
that the checks I contend for in the system proposed, do not, in the least, any
of them tend to lessen the energy of it; but giving grounds for the confidence

of the people, greatly to increase its real energy, by insuring their constant and hearty support.

The FEDERAL FARMER.

XI

The Senate

JANUARY 10, 1788.

DEAR SIR,

I SHALL now add a few observations respecting the organization of the senate, the manner of appointing it, and its powers.

The senate is an assembly of 26 members, two from each state, though the senators are apportioned on the federal plan, they will vote individually; they represent the states, as bodies politic, sovereign to certain purposes; the states being sovereign and independent, are all considered equal, each with the other in the senate. In this we are governed solely by the ideal equalities of sovereignties; the federal and state governments forming one whole, and the state governments an essential part, which ought always to be kept distinctly in view, and preserved: I feel more disposed, on reflection, to acquiesce in making them the basis of the senate, and thereby to make it the interest and duty of the senators to preserve distinct, and to perpetuate the respective sovereignties they shall represent.

As to the appointments of senators, I have already observed, that they must be appointed by the legislatures, by concurrent acts, and each branch have an equal share of power, as I do not see any probability of amendments, if advisable, in these points, I shall not dwell upon them.

The senate, as a legislative branch, is not large, but as an executive branch quite too numerous. It is not to be presumed that we can form a genuine senatorial branch in the United States, a real representation of the aristocracy and balance in the legislature, any more than we can form a genuine representation of the people. Could we separate the aristocratical and democratical interests; compose the senate of the former, and the house of assembly of the latter, they are too unequal in the United States to produce a balance. Form them on pure principles, and leave each to be supported by its real weight and connections, the senate would be feeble, and the house powerful:—I say, on pure principles; because I make a distinction between a senate that derives its weight and influence from a pure source, its numbers and wisdom, its extensive property, its extensive and permanent connections; and a senate composed of a few men, possessing small property, small and unstable connections, that derives its weight and influence from a corrupt or pernicious source; that is, merely from the power given it by the constitution and laws, to dispose of the public offices, and the annexed emoluments, and by those means to interest officers, and the hungry expectants of offices, in support of its measures. I wish the proposed senate may not partake too much of the latter description.

To produce a balance and checks, the constitution proposes two branches in the legislature; but they are so formed, that the members of both must generally be the same kind of men—men having similar interests and views, feelings and connections—men of the same grade in society, and who associate on all occasions (probably, if there be any difference, the senators will be the most democratic). Senators and representatives thus circumstanced, as men, though convened in two rooms, to make laws, must be governed generally by the same motives and views, and therefore pursue the same system of politics; the partitions between the two branches will be merely those of the building in which they sit: there will not be found in them any of those genuine balances and checks, among the real different interests, and efforts of the several classes of men in the community we aim at; nor can any such balances and checks be formed in the present condition of the United States in any considerable degree of perfection: but to give them the greatest degree of perfection practicable, we ought to make the senate respectable as to numbers, the qualifications of the electors and of the elected; to increase the numbers of the representatives, and so to model the elections of them, as always to draw a majority of them substantially from the body of the people. Though I conclude the senators and representatives will not form in the legislature those balances and checks which correspond with the actual state of the people; yet I approve of two branches, because we may notwithstanding derive several advantages from them. The senate, from the mode of its appointment, will probably be influenced to support the state governments, and, from its periods of service will produce stability in legislation, while frequent elections may take place in the other branch. There is generally a degree of competition between two assemblies even composed of the same kind of men; and by this, and by means of every law's passing a revision in the second branch, caution, coolness, and deliberation are produced in the business of making laws. By means of a democratic branch we may particularly secure personal liberty; and by means of a senatorial branch we may particularly protect property. By the division, the house becomes the proper body to impeach all officers for misconduct in office, and the senate the proper court to try them; and in a country where limited powers must be lodged in the first magistrate, the senate, perhaps, may be the most proper body to be found to have a negative upon him in making treaties, and in managing foreign affairs.

Though I agree the federal senate, in the form proposed, may be useful to many purposes, and that it is not very necessary to alter the organization, modes of appointment, and powers of it in several respects; yet, without alterations in others, I sincerely believe it will, in a very few years, become the source of the greatest evils. Some of these alterations, I conceive, to be absolutely necessary, and some of them at least advisable.

1. By the confederation the members of congress are chosen annually. By art. 1. sect. 2. of the constitution, the senators shall be chosen for six years. As the period of service must be, in a considerable degree, matter of opinion on this head, I shall only make a few observations, to explain why I think it more advisable to limit it to three or four years.

The people of this country have not been accustomed to so long appointments in their state governments, they have generally adopted annual elections. The members of the present congress are chosen yearly, who, from the nature and multiplicity of their business, ought to be chosen for longer periods then the federal senators—Men six years in office absolutely contract callous habits, and cease, in too great a degree, to feel their dependance, and for the condition of their constituents. Senators continued in offices three or four years, will be in them longer than any popular erroneous opinions will probably continue to actuate their electors—men appointed for three or four years, will generally be long enough in office to give stability, and amply to acquire political information. By a change of legislators, as often as circumstances will permit, political knowledge is diffused more extensively among the people, and the attention of the electors and elected more constantly kept alive; circumstances of infinite importance in a free country. Other reasons might be added, but my subject is too extensive to admit of my dwelling upon less material points.

2. When the confederation was formed, it was considered essentially necessary that the members of congress should at any time be recalled by their respective states, when the states should see fit, and others be sent in their room. I do not think it less necessary that this principle should be extended to the members of congress under the new constitution, and especially to the senators. I have had occasion several times to observe, that let us form a federal constitution as extensively, and on the best principles in our power, we must, after all, trust a vast deal to a few men, who, far removed from their constituents, will administer the federal government; there is but little danger these men will feel too great a degree of dependance: the necessary and important object to be attended to, is to make them feel dependant enough. Men elected for several years, several hundred miles distant from their states, possessed of very extensive powers, and the means of paying themselves, will not, probably, be oppressed with a sense of dependance and responsibility.

The senators will represent sovereignties, which generally have, and always ought to retain, the power of recalling their agents; the principle of responsibility is strongly felt in men who are liable to be recalled and censured for their misconduct; and, if we may judge from experience, the latter will not abuse the power of recalling their members; to possess it, will, at least be a valuable check. It is in the nature of all delegated power, that the constituents should retain the right to judge concerning the conduct of their representatives; they must exercise the power, and their decision itself, their approving or disapproving that conduct implies a right, a power to continue in office, or to remove from it. But whenever the substitute acts under a constitution, then it becomes necessary that the power of recalling him be expressed. The reasons for lodging a power to recall are stronger, as they respect the senate, than as they respect the representatives; the latter will be more frequently elected, and changed of course, and being chosen by the people at large, it would be more difficult for the people than for the legislatures to take the necessary measures for recalling: but even the people, if the power will be more beneficial to them than injurious, ought to possess it. The people are not apt to wrong a man who is steady and true to their interests; they may for a while be misled by party representations, and leave a good man out of office unheard; but every recall supposes a deliberate decision, and a fair hearing; and no man who believes his conduct proper, and the result of honest views, will be the less useful in his public character, on account of the examination his actions may be liable to; and a man conscious of the contrary conduct, ought clearly to be restrained by the apprehensions of a trial. I repeat it, it is interested combinations and factions we are particularly to guard against in the federal government, and all the rational means that can be put into the hands of the people to prevent them, ought to be provided and furnished for them. Where there is a power to recall, trusty centinels among the people, or in the state legislatures, will have a fair opportunity to become useful. If the members in congress from the states join in such combinations, or favour them, or pursue a pernicious line of conduct; the most attentive among the people, or in the state legislatures, may formally charge them before their constituents: the very apprehensions of such constitutional charges may prevent many of the evils mentioned, and the recalling the members of a single state, a single senator, or representative, may often prevent many more; nor do I, at present, discover any danger in such proceedings, as every man who shall move for a recall will put his reputation at stake, to shew he has reasonable grounds for his motion; and it is not probable such motions will be made unless there be good apparent grounds for succeeding; nor can the charge or motion be any thing more than the attack of an individual or individuals, unless a majority of the constituents shall see cause to go into the enquiry. Further, the circumstance of such a power being lodged in the constituents, will tend continually to keep up their watchfulness, as well as the attention and dependance of the federal senators and representatives.

3. By the confederation it is provided, that no delegate shall serve more than three years in any term of six years, and thus, by the forms of the government, a rotation of members is produced: a like principle has been adopted in some of the state governments, and also in some antient and modern republics. Whether this exclusion of a man for a given period, after

he shall have served a given time, ought to be ingrafted into a constitution or not, is a question, the proper decision materially depends upon the leading features of the government: some governments are so formed as to produce a sufficient fluctuation and change of members of course, in the ordinary course of elections, proper numbers of new members are, from time to time, brought into the legislature, and a porportionate number of old ones go out, mix, and become diffused among the people. This is the case with all numerous representative legislatures, the members of which are frequently elected, and constantly within the view of their constituents. This is the case with our state governments, and in them a constitutional rotation is unimportant. But in a government consisting of but a few members, elected for long periods, and far removed from the observation of the people, but few changes in the ordinary course of elections take place among the members; they become in some measure a fixed body, and often inattentive to the public good, callous, selfish, and the fountain of corruption. To prevent these evils, and to force a principle of pure animation into the federal government, which will be formed much in this last manner mentioned, and to produce attention, activity, and a diffusion of knowledge in the community, we ought to establish among others the principle of rotation. Even good men in office, in time, imperceptibly lose sight of the people, and gradually fall into measures prejudicial to them. It is only a rotation among the members of the federal legislature I shall contend for: judges and officers at the heads of the judicial and executive departments, are in a very different situation, their offices and duties require the information and studies of many years for performing them in a manner advantageous to the people. These judges and officers must apply their whole time to the detail business of their offices, and depend on them for their support; then they always act under masters or superiors, and may be removed from office for misconduct; they pursue a certain round of executive business: their offices must be in all societies confined to a few men, because but few can become qualified to fill them: and were they, by annual appointments, open to the people at large, they are offices of such a nature as to be of no service to them; they must leave these offices in the possession of the few individuals qualified to fill them, or have them badly filled. In the judicial and executive departments also, the body of the people possess a large share of power and influence, as jurors and subordinate officers, among whom there are many and frequent rotations. But in every free country the legislatures are all on a level, and legislation becomes partial whenever, in practice, it rests for any considerable time in a few hands. It is the true republican principle to diffuse the power of making the laws among the people, and so to modify the forms of the government as to draw in turn the well informed of every class into the legislature.

To determine the propriety or impropriety of this rotation, we must take the inconveniencies as well as the advantages attending it into view: on the one hand, by this rotation, we may sometimes exclude good men from being elected. On the other hand, we guard against those pernicious connections, which usually grow up among men left to continue long periods in office, we increase the number of those who make the laws and return to their constituents; and thereby spread information, and preserve a spirit of activity and investigation among the people: hence a balance of interests and exertions are preserved, and the ruinous measures of factions rendered more impracticable. I would not urge the principle of rotation, if I believed the consequence would be an uninformed federal legislature; but I have no apprehension of this in this enlightened country. The members of congress, at any one time, must be but very few, compared with the respectable well informed men in the United States; and I have no idea there will be any want of such men for members of congress, though by a principle of rotation the constitution should exclude from being elected for two years those federal legislators, who may have served the four years immediately preceding, or any four years in the six preceding years. If we may judge from experience and fair calculations, this principle will never operate to exclude at any one period a fifteenth part, even of those men who have been members of congress. Though no man can sit in congress, by the confederation, more than three years in any term of six years, yet not more than three, four, or five men in any one state, have been made ineligible at any one period; and if a good man happen to be excluded by this rotation, it is only for a short time. All things considered, the inconveniencies of the principle must be very inconsiderable compared with the many advantages of it. It will generally be expedient for a man who has served four years in congress to return home, mix with the people, and reside some time with them: this will tend to reinstate him in the interests, feelings, and views similar to theirs, and thereby confirm in him the essential qualifications of a legislator. Even in point of information, it may be observed, the useful information of legislators is not acquired merely in studies in offices, and in meeting to make laws from day to day; they must learn the actual situation of the people, by being among them, and when they have made laws, return home, and observe how they operate. Thus occasionally to be among the people, is not only necessary to prevent or banish the callous habits and self-interested views of office in legislators, but to afford them necessary information, and to render them useful: another valuable end is answered by it, sympathy, and the means of communication between them and their constituents, is substantially promoted; so that on every principle legislators, at certain periods, ought to live among their constituents.

Some men of science are undoubtedly necessary in every legislature; but the knowledge, generally, necessary for men who make laws, is a knowledge of the common concerns, and particular circumstances of the people. In a republican government seats in the legislature are highly honorable; I believe but few do, and surely none ought to consider them as places of profit and permanent support. Were the people always properly attentive, they would, at proper periods, call their law makers home, by sending others in their room: but this is not often the case, and therefore, in making constitutions, when the people are attentive, they ought cautiously to provide for those benefits, those advantageous changes in the administration of their affairs, which they are often apt to be inattentive to in practice. On the whole, to guard against the evils, and to secure the advantages I have mentioned, with the greatest degree of certainty, we ought clearly, in my opinion, to increase the federal representation, to secure elections on proper principles, to establish a right to recall members, and a rotation among them.

4. By the art. 2. sect. 2. treaties must be made with the advice and consent of the senate, and two-thirds of those present must concur: also, with consent of the senate, almost all federal officers, civil and military, must be appointed. As to treaties I have my doubts, but as to the appointments of officers, I think we may clearly shew the senate to be a very improper body indeed to have any thing to do with them. I am not perfectly satisfied, that the senate, a branch of the legislature, and court for trying impeachments, ought to have a controuling power in making all treaties; yet, I confess, I do not discern how a restraint upon the president in this important business, can be better or more safely lodged: a power to make and conclude all treaties is too important to be vested in him alone, or in him and an executive council, only sufficiently numerous for other purpose, and the house of representatives is too numerous to be concerned in treaties of peace and of alliance. This power is now lodged in congress, to be exercised by the consent of nine states. The federal senate, like the delegations in the present congress, will represent the states, and the consent of two-thirds of that senate will bear some similitude to the consent of nine states. It is probable the United States will not make more than one treaty, on an average, in two or three years, and this power may always be exercised with great deliberation: perhaps the senate is sufficiently numerous to be trusted with this power, sufficiently small to proceed with secrecy, and sufficiently permanent to exercise this power with proper consistency and due deliberation. To lodge this power in a less respectable and less numerous body might not be safe; we must place great confidence in the hands that hold it, and we deceive ourselves if we give it under an idea, that we can impeach, to any valuable purpose, the man or men who may abuse it.

On a fair construction of the constitution, I think the legislature has a proper controul over the president and senate in settling commercial treaties. By art. 1. sect. 2. the legislature will have power to regulate commerce with foreign nations, &c. By art. 2. sect. 2. the president, with the advice and consent of two-thirds of the senate, may make treaties. These clauses must be considered together, and we ought never to make one part of the same instrument contradict another, if it can be avoided by any reasonable construction. By the first recited clause, the legislature has the power, that is, as I understand it, the sole power to regulate commerce with foreign nations, or to make all the rules and regulations respecting trade and commerce between our citizens and foreigners: by the second recited clause, the president and senate have power generally to make treaties.—There are several kinds of treaties—as treaties of commerce, of peace, of alliance, &c. I think the words to "make treaties," may be consistently construed, and yet so as it shall be left to the legislature to confirm commercial treaties; they are in their nature and operation very distinct from treaties of peace and of alliance; the latter generally require secrecy, it is but very seldom they interfere with the laws and internal police of the country; to make them is properly the exercise of executive powers and the constitution authorises the president and senate to make treaties, and gives the legislature no power, directly or indirectly, respecting these treaties of peace and alliance. As to treaties of commerce, they do not generally require secrecy, they almost always involve in them legislative powers, interfere with the laws and internal police of the country, and operate immediately on persons and property, especially in the commercial towns: (they have in Great-Britain usually been confirmed by parliament;) they consist of rules and regulations respecting commerce; and to regulate commerce, or to make regulations respecting commerce, the federal legislature, by the constitution, has the power. I do not see that any commercial regulations can be made in treaties, that will not infringe upon this power in the legislature; therefore, I infer, that the true construction is, that the president and senate shall make treaties, but all commercial treaties shall be subject to be confirmed by the legislature. This construction will render the clauses consistent, and make the powers of the president and senate, respecting treaties, much less exceptionable.

The FEDERAL FARMER.

XII

The Regulation of Elections

JANUARY 12, 1788.

DEAR SIR,

ON carefully examining the parts of the proposed system, respecting the elections of senators, and especially of the representatives, they appear to me to be both ambiguous and very defective. I shall endeavour to pursue a course of reasoning, which shall fairly lead to establishing the impartiality and security of elections, and then to point out an amendment in this respect.

It is well observed by Montesquieu, that in republican governments, the forms of elections are fundamental; and that it is an essential part of the social compact, to ascertain by whom, to whom, when, and in what manner suffrages are to be given.

Wherever we find the regulation of elections have not been carefully fixed by the constitution, or the principles of them, we constantly see the legislatures new modifying its own form, and changing the spirit of the government to answer partial purposes.

By the proposed plan it is fixed, that the qualifications of the electors of the federal representatives shall be the same as those of the electors of state representatives; though these vary some in the several states the electors are fixed and designated.

The qualifications of the representatives are also fixed and designated, and no person under 25 years of age, not an inhabitant of the state, and not having been seven years a citizen of the United States, can be elected; the clear inference is, that all persons 25 years of age, and upwards, inhabitants of the state, and having been, at any period or periods, seven years citizens of the United States, may be elected representatives. They have a right to be elected by the constitution, and the electors have a right to chuse them. This is fixing the federal representation, as to the elected, on a very broad basis: it can be no objection to the elected, that they are Christians, Pagans, Mahometans, or Jews; that they are of any colour, rich or poor, convict or not: Hence many men may be elected, who cannot be electors. Gentlemen who have commented so largely upon the wisdom of the constitution, for excluding from being elected young men under a certain age, would have done well to have recollected, that it positively makes pagans, convicts, &c. eligible. The people make the constitution; they exclude a few persons, by certain descriptions, from being elected, and all not thus excluded are clearly admitted. Now a man 25 years old, an inhabitant of the state, and having been a citizen of the states seven years, though afterwards convicted, may be elected, because not within any of the excluding clauses; the same of a beggar, an absentee, &c.

The right of the electors, and eligibility of the elected being fixed by the people, they cannot be narrowed by the state legislatures, or congress: it is established, that a man being (among other qualifications) an inhabitant of the state, shall be eligible. Now it would be narrowing the right of the people to confine them in their choice to a man, an inhabitant of a particular county or district in the state. Hence it follows, that neither the state legislatures or congress can establish district elections; that is, divide the state into districts, and confine the electors of each district to the choice of a man resident in it. If the electors could be thus limited in one respect, they might in another be confined to chuse a man of a particular religion, of certain property, &c. and thereby half of the persons made eligible by the constitution be excluded. All laws, therefore, for regulating elections must be made on the broad basis of the constitution.

Next, we may observe, that representatives are to be chosen by the people of the state. What is a choice by the people of the state? If each given district in it choose one, will that be a choice within the meaning of the constitution?

Must the choice be by plurality of votes, or a majority? In connection with these questions, we must take the 4th sect. art. 1. where it is said the state legislatures shall prescribe the times, places, and manner of holding elections; but congress may make or alter such regulations. By this clause, I suppose, the electors of different towns and districts in the state may be assembled in different places, to give their votes; but when so assembled, by another clause they cannot, by congress or the state legislatures, be restrained from giving their votes for any man an inhabitant of the state, and qualified as to age, and having been a citizen the time required. But I see nothing in the constitution by which to decide, whether the choice shall be by a plurality or a majority of votes: this, in my mind, is by far the most important question in the business of elections. When we say a representative shall be chosen by the people, it seems to imply that he shall be chosen by a majority of them; but states which use the same phraseology in this respect, practice both ways. I believe a majority of the states, chuse by pluralities, and, I think it probable, that the federal house of representatives will decide that a choice of its members by pluralities is constitutional. A man who has the most votes is chosen in Great-Britain. It is this, among other things, that gives every man fair play in the game of influence and corruption. I believe that not much stress was laid upon the objection that congress may assemble the electors at some out of the way place. However, the advocates seem to think they obtain a victory of no small glory and importance, when they can shew, with some degree of colour, that the evils are rather a possibility than a probability.

When I observed that the elections were not secured on proper principles, I had an idea of far more probable and extensive evils, secret mischiefs, and not so glaring transgressions, the exclusions of proper district elections, and of the choice by a majority.

It is easy to perceive that there is an essential difference between elections by pluralities and by majorities, between choosing a man in a small or limited district, and choosing a number of men promiscuously by the people of a large state; and while we are almost secure of judicious unbiassed elections by majorities in such districts, we have no security against deceptions, influence and corruption in states or large districts in electing by pluralities. When a choice is made by a plurality of votes, it is often made by a very small part of the electors, who attend and give their votes, when by a majority never by so few as one half of them. The partialities and improprieties attending the former mode may be illustrated by a case that lately happened in one of the middle states.—Several representatives were to be chosen by a large number of inhabitants compactly settled, among whom there were four or five thousand voters. Previous to the time of election a number of lists of candidates were published, to divide and distract the voters in general— about half a dozen men of some influence, who had a favourite list to carry, met several times, fixed their list, and agreed to hand it about among all who could probably be induced to adopt it, and to circulate the other lists among their opponents, to divide them. The poll was opened, and several hundred electors, suspecting nothing, attended and put in their votes; the list of the half dozen was carried, and men were found to be chosen, some of whom were very disagreeable to a large majority of the electors: though several hundred electors voted, men on that list were chosen who had only 45, 43, 44, &c. votes each; they had a plurality, that is, more than any other persons: the votes generally were scattered, and those who made even a feeble combination succeeded in placing highest upon the list several very unthought of and very unpopular men. This evil never could have happened in a town where all the voters meet in one place, and consider no man as elected unless he have a majority, or more than half of all the votes; clear it is, that the men on whom thus but a small part of the votes are bestowed, cannot possess the confidence of the people, or have any considerable degree of influence over them.

But as partial, as liable to secret influence, and corruption as the choice by pluralities may be, I think, we cannot avoid it, without essentially increasing the federal representation, and adopting the principles of district elections. There is but one case in which the choice by the majority is practicable, and that is, where districts are formed of such moderate extent that the electors in each can conveniently meet in one place, and at one time, and proceed to the choice of a representative; when, if no man have a majority, or more than half of all the votes the first time, the voters may examine the characters of those brought forward, accommodate, and proceed to repeat their votes till some one shall have that majority. This, I believe, cannot be a case under the constitution proposed in its present form. To explain my ideas, take Massachusetts, for instance, she is entitled to eight representatives, she has 370,000 inhabitants, about 46,000 to one representative; if the elections be so held that the electors throughout the state meet in their several towns or places, and each elector puts in his vote for eight representatives, the votes of the electors will ninety-nine times in a hundred, be so scattered that on collecting the votes from the several towns or places, no men will be found, each of whom have a majority of the votes, and therefore the election will not be made. On the other hand, there may be such a combination of votes, that in thus attempting to chuse eight representatives, the electors may chuse even fifteen. Suppose 10,000 voters to attend and give their votes, each voter will give eight votes, one for each of eight representatives; in the whole 80,000 votes will be given—eight men, each having 5001 votes, in the whole 40,008 will have each a majority, and be chosen—39,092 votes will be bestowed on other men, and if they all be bestowed on seven men, they may have each a considerable majority, and also be chosen. This indeed is a very rare combination: but the bestowing all the votes pretty equally upon nine, ten, or eleven men, and chusing them all, is an event too probable not to be guarded against.

If Massachusetts be divided into eight districts, each having about 46,000 inhabitants, and each district directed to chuse one representative, it will be found totally impracticable for the electors of it to meet in one place; and, when they meet in several towns and places in the district, they will vote for different men, and nineteen times in twenty, so scatter their votes, that no one man will have a majority of the whole and be chosen: we must, therefore, take the man who has the most votes, whether he has three quarters, one quarter, or one tenth part of the whole; the inconveniencies of scattering votes will be increased, as men not of the district, as well as those that are in it, may be voted for.

I might add many other observations to evince the superiority and solid advantages of proper district elections, and a choice by a majority, and to prove, that many evils attend the contrary practice: these evils we must encounter as the constitution now stands.

I see no way to fix elections on a proper footing, and to render tolerably equal and secure the federal representation, but by increasing the representation, so as to have one representative for each district, in which the electors may conveniently meet in one place, and at one time, and chuse by a majority. Perhaps this might be effected pretty generally, by fixing one representative for each twelve thousand inhabitants; dividing, or fixing the principles for dividing the states into proper districts; and directing the electors of each district to the choice, by a majority, of some men having a permanent interest and residence in it. I speak of a representation tolerably equal, &c. because I am still of opinion, that it is impracticable in this extensive country to have a federal representation sufficiently democratic, or substantially drawn from the body of the people: the principles just mentioned may be the best practical ones we can expect to establish. By thus increasing the representation, we not only make it more democratical and secure, strengthen the confidence of the people in it, and thereby render it more nervous and energetic; but it will also enable the people essentially to change, for the better, the principles and forms of elections. To provide for the people's wandering throughout the state for a representative, may sometimes enable them to elect a more brilliant or an abler man, than by confining them to districts, but generally this latitude will be used to pernicious purposes, especially connected with the choice by plurality; when a man in the remote part of the state, perhaps, obnoxious at home, but ambitious and intriguing, may be chosen to represent the people in another part of the state far distant, and by a small part of them, or by a faction, or by a combination of some particular description of men among them. This has been long the case in Great-Britain, it is the case in several of the states, nor do I think that such pernicious practices will be merely possible in our federal concerns, but highly probable. By establishing district elections, we exclude none of the best men from being elected; and we fix what, in my mind, is of far more importance than brilliant talents, I mean a sameness, as to residence and interests, between the representative and his constituents; and by the election by a majority, he is sure to be the man, the choice of more than half of them.

Though it is impossible to put elections on a proper footing as the constitution stands, yet I think regulations respecting them may be introduced of considerable service: it is not only, therefore, important to enquire how they may be made, but also what body has the controuling power over them. An intelligent, free and unbiassed choice of representatives by the people is of the last importance: we must then carefully guard against all combinations, secret arts, and influence to the contrary. Various expedients have been adopted in different countries and states to effect genuine elections; as the constitution now stands, I confess, I do not discover any better than those adopted in Connecticut, in the choice of counsellers, before mentioned.

The federal representatives are to be chosen every second year (an odd mode of expression). In all the states, except South-Carolina, the people, the same electors, meet twice in that time to elect state representatives. For instance, let the electors in Massachusetts, when they meet to chuse state representatives, put in their votes for eight federal representatives, the number that state may chuse, (merely for distinction sake, we may call these the votes of nomination), and return a list of the men voted for, in the several towns and places, to the legislature, or some proper body; let this list be immediately examined and published, and some proper number, say 15 or 20, who shall have the most votes upon the list, be sent out to the people; and when the electors shall meet the next year to chuse state representatives, let them put in their votes for the eight federal representatives, confining their votes to the proper number so sent out; and let the eight highest of those thus voted for in the two votes (which we may call, by way of distinction, votes of election), be the federal representatives: thus a choice may be made by the people, once in two years, without much trouble and expence, and, I believe, with some degree of security. As soon as the votes of nomination shall be collected and made known, the people will know who are voted for, and who are candidates for their votes the succeeding year; the electors will have near a year to enquire into their characters and politics, and also into any undue means, if any were taken, to bring any of them forward; and such as they find to be the best men, and agreeable to the people, they may vote for in giving the votes of election. By these means the men chosen will ultimately always have a majority, or near a majority, of the votes of the electors, who shall attend and give their votes. The mode itself will lead to the discovery of truth and of political characters, and to prevent private combinations, by rendering them in a great measure of no effect. As the choice is to be made by the people, all combinations and checks must be confined to their votes. No supplying the want of a majority by the legislatures, as in Massachusetts in the choice of senators, &c. can be admitted: the people generally judge right when informed, and, in giving their votes the second time, they may always correct their former errors.

I think we are all sufficiently acquainted with the progress of elections to see, that the regulations, as to times, places, and the manner merely of holding elections, may, under the constitution, easily be made useful or injurious. It is important then to enquire, who has the power to make regulations, and who ought to have it. By the constitution, the state legislatures shall prescribe the times, places, and manner of holding elections, but congress may make or alter such regulations. Power in congress merely to alter those regulations, made by the states, could answer no valuable purposes; the states might make, and congress alter them *ad infinitum;* and when the state should cease to make, or should annihilate its regulations, congress would have nothing to alter. But the states shall make regulations, and congress may make such regulations as the clause stands: the true construction is, that when congress shall see fit to regulate the times, places, and manner of holding elections, congress may do it, and state regulations, on this head, must cease: for if state regulations could exist, after congress should make a system of regulations, there would, or might, be two incompatible systems of regulations relative to the same subject.

It has been often urged, that congress ought to have power to make these regulations, otherwise the state legislatures, by neglecting to make provision for elections, or by making improper regulations, may destroy the general government. It is very improbable that any state legislature will adopt measures to destroy the representation of its own constituents in congress, especially when the state must, represented in congress or not, pay its proportion of the expence of keeping up the government, and even of the representatives of the other states, and be subject to their laws. Should the state legislatures be disposed to be negligent, or to combine to break up congress, they have a very simple way to do it, as the constitution now stands—they have only to neglect to chuse senators, or to appoint the electors of the president, and vice-president: there is no remedy provided against these last evils: nor is it to be presumed, that if a sufficient number of state legislatures to break up congress, should, by neglect or otherwise, attempt to do it, that the people, who yearly elect those legislatures, would elect under the regulations of congress. These and many other reasons must evince, that it was not merely to prevent an annihilation of the federal government that congress has power to regulate elections.

It has been urged also, that the state legislatures chuse the federal senators, one branch, and may injure the people, who chuse the other, by improper regulations; that therefore congress, in which the people will immediately have one, the representative branch, ought to have power to interfere in behalf of the people, and rectify such improper regulations. The advocates have said much about the opponents dwelling upon possibilities; but to suppose the people will find it necessary to appeal to congress to restrain the oppressions of the state legislatures, is supposing a possibility indeed. Can any man in his senses suppose that the state legislatures, which are so numerous as almost to be the people themselves, all branches of them depending yearly, for the most part, on the elections of the people, will abuse them in regulating federal elections, and make it proper to transfer the power to congress, a body, one branch of which is chosen once in six years by these very legislatures, and the other biennially and not half so numerous as even the senatorial branches in those legislatures?

Senators are to be chosen by the state legislatures, where there are two branches the appointment must be, I presume, by a concurrent resolution, in passing which, as in passing all other legislative acts, each branch will have a negative; this will give the senatorial branch just as much weight in the appointment as the democratic: the two branches form a legislature only when acting separately, and therefore, whenever the members of the two branches meet, mix and vote individually in one room, for making an election, it is expressly so directed by the constitutions. If the constitution, by fixing the choice to be made by the legislatures, has given each branch an equal vote, as I think it has, it cannot be altered by any regulations.

On the whole, I think, all general principles respecting electors ought to be carefully established by the constitution, as the qualifications of the electors and of elected: the number of the representatives, and the inhabitants of each given district, called on to chuse a man from among themselves by a majority of votes; leaving it to the legislature only so to regulate, from time to time, the extent of the districts so as to keep the representatives proportionate to the number of inhabitants in the several parts of the country; and so far as regulations as to elections cannot be fixed by the constitution, they ought to be left to the state legislatures, they coming far nearest to the people themselves; at most, congress ought to have power to regulate elections only where a state shall neglect to make them.

The FEDERAL FARMER.

XIII

The Executive Branch I

JANUARY 14, 1788.

DEAR SIR,

IN this letter I shall further examine two clauses in the proposed consitution respecting appointments to office—By art. 2. sect. 2. the president shall nominate, and by and with the advice and consent of the senate, shall appoint ambassadors, other public ministers and consuls, judges of the supreme court, and all other officers of the United States, whose appointments, &c. By art. 1, sect. 6. No senator or representative shall, during the term for which he was elected, be appointed to any civil office under the authority of the United States, which shall have been created, or the emoluments whereof shall have been increased during such time.

Thus the president must nominate, and the senate concur in the appointment of all federal officers, civil and military, and the senators and representatives are made ineligible only to the few civil offices abovementioned. To preserve the federal government pure and uncorrupt, peculiar precautions relative to appointments to office will be found highly necessary from the very forms and character of the government itself. The honours and emoluments of public offices are the objects in all communities, that ambitious and necessitous men never lose sight of. The honest, the modest, and the industrious part of the community content themselves, generally, with their private concerns; they do not solicit those offices which are the perpetual source of cabals, intrigues, and contests among men of the former description, men embarrassed, intriguing, and destitute of modesty. Even in the most happy country and virtuous government, corrupt influence in appointments cannot always be avoided; perhaps we may boast of our share of virtue as a people, and if we are only sufficiently aware of the influence, biasses, and prejudices, common to the affairs of men, we may go far towards guarding against the effects of them.

We all agree, that a large standing army has a strong tendency to depress and inslave the people; it is equally true that a large body of selfish, unfeeling, unprincipled civil officers has a like, or a more pernicious tendency to the same point. Military and especially civil establishments, are the necessary appendages of society; they are deductions from productive labour, and substantial wealth, in proportion to the number of men employed in them; they are oppressive where unnecessarily extended and supported by men unfriendly to the people; they are injurious when too small, and supported by men too timid and dependant. It is of the last importance to decide well upon the necessary number of offices, to fill them with proper characters, and to establish efficiently the means of punctually punishing those officers who may do wrong.

To discern the nature and extent of this power of appointments, we need only to consider the vast number of officers necessary to execute a national system in this extensive country, the prodigious biasses the hopes and expectations of offices have on their conduct, and the influence public officers have among the people—these necessary officers, as judges, state's attornies, clerks, sheriffs, &c. in the federal supreme and inferior courts, admirals and generals, and subordinate officers in the army and navy, ministers, consuls, &c. sent to foreign countries; officers in the federal city, in the revenue, post office departments, &c. &c. must, probably, amount to several thousands, without taking into view the very inferior ones. There can be no doubt but that the most active men in politics, in and out of congress, will be the foremost candidates for the best of these offices; the man or men who shall have the disposal of them, beyond dispute, will have by far the greatest share of active influence in the government; but appointments must be made, and who shall make them? what modes of appointments will be attended with the fewest inconveniencies? is the question. The senators and representatives are the law makers, create all offices, and whenever they see fit, they impeach and try officers for misconduct; they ought to be in session but part of the year, and as legislators, they must be too numerous to make appointments, perhaps, a few very important ones excepted. In contemplating the necessary officers of the union, there appear to be six different modes in which, in whole or in part, the appointments may be made, 1. By the legislature; 2. by the president and senate— 3. by the president and an executive council— 4. by the president alone— 5. by the heads of the departments—and 6. by the state governments—Among all these, in my opinion, there may be an advantageous distribution of the power of appointments. In considering the legislators, in relation to the subject before us, two interesting questions particularly arise— 1. Whether they ought to be eligible to any offices whatever during the period for which they shall be elected to serve, and even for some time afterwards—and 2. How far they ought to participate in the power of appointments. As to the first, it is true that legislators in foreign countries, or in our state governments, are not generally made ineligible to office: there are good reasons for it; in many countries the people have gone on without ever examining the principles of government. There have been but few countries in which the legislators have been a particular set of men periodically chosen: but the principal reason is, that which operates in the several states, viz. the legislators are so frequently chosen, and so numerous, compared with the number of offices for which they can reasonably consider themselves as candidates, that the chance of any individual member's being chosen, is too small to raise his hopes or expectations, or to have any considerable influence upon his conduct. Among the state legislators, one man in twenty may be appointed in some committee business, &c. for a month or two; but on a fair computation, not one man in a hundred sent to the state legislatures is appointed to any permanent office of profit: directly the reverse of this will evidently be found true in the federal administration. Throughout the United States, about four federal senators, and thirty-three representatives, averaging the elections, will be chosen in a year; these few men may rationally consider themselves as the fairest candidates for a very great number of lucrative offices, which must become vacant in the year, and pretty clearly a majority of the federal legislators, if not excluded, will be mere expectants for public offices. I need not adduce further arguments to establish a position so clear; I need only call to your recollection my observations in a former letter, wherein I endeavoured to shew the fallacy of the argument, that the members must return home and mix with the people. It is said, that men are governed by interested motives, and will not attend as legislators, unless they can, in common with others, be eligible to offices of honor and profit. This will undoubtedly be the case with some men, but I presume only with such men as never ought to be chosen legislators in a free country; an opposite principle will influence good men; virtuous patriots, and generous minds, will esteem it a higher honor to be selected as the guardians of a free people; they will be satisfied with a reasonable compensation for their time and service; nor will they wish to be within the vortex of influence. The valuable effects of this principle of making legislators ineligible to offices for a given time, has never yet been sufficiently attended to or considered: I am assured, that it was established by the convention after long debate, and afterwards, on an unfortunate change of a few members, altered. Could the federal legislators be excluded in the manner proposed, I think it would be an important point gained; as to themselves, they would be left to act much more from motives consistent with the public good.

In considering the principle of rotation I had occasion to distinguish the condition of a legislator from that of mere official man—We acquire certain habits, feelings, and opinions, as men and citizens—others, and very different ones, from a long continuance in office: It is, therefore, a valuable observation in many bills of rights, that rulers ought frequently to return and mix with the people. A legislature, in a free country, must be numerous; it is in some degree a periodical assemblage of the people, frequently formed—the principal officers in the executive and judicial departments, must have more permanency in office. Hence it may be inferred, that the legislature will remain longer uncorrupted and virtuous; longer congenial to the people, than the officers of those departments. If it is not, therefore, in our power to preserve republican principles, for a series of ages, in all the departments of government, we may a long while preserve them in a well formed legislature. To this end we ought to take every precaution to prevent legislators becoming mere office-men; chuse them frequently, make them recallable, establish rotation among them, make them ineligible to offices, and give them as small a share as possible in the disposal of them. Add to this, a legislature, in the nature of things, is not formed for the detail business of appointing officers; there is also generally an impropriety in the same men's making offices and filling them, and a still greater impropriety in their impeaching and trying the officers they appoint. For these, and other reasons, I conclude the legislature is not a proper body for the appointment of officers in general. But having gone through with the different modes of appointment, I shall endeavour to shew what share in the distribution of the power of appointments the legislature must, from necessity, rather than from propriety, take. 2. Officers may be appointed by the president and senate—this mode, for general purposes, is clearly not defensible. All the reasoning touching the legislature will apply to the senate; the senate is a branch of the legislature, which ought to be kept pure and unbiassed; it has a part in trying officers for misconduct, and in creating offices, it is too numerous for a council of appointment, or to feel any degree of responsibility; if it has an advantage of the legislature, in being the least numerous, it has a disadvantage in being more unsafe: add to this, the senate is to have a share in the important branch of power respecting treaties. Further, this sexennial senate of 26 members, representing 13 sovereign states, will not, in practice, be found to be a body to advise, but to order and dictate in fact; and the president will be a mere *primus inter pares.* The consequence will be, that the senate, with these efficient means of influence, will not only dictate, probably, to the president, but manage the house, as the constitution now stands; and under appearances of a balanced system, in reality, govern alone. There may also, by this undue connection, be particular periods when a very popular president may have a very improper influence upon the senate and upon the legislature. A council of appointment must very probably sit all, or near all, the year—the senate will be too important and too expensive a body for this. By giving the senate, directly or indirectly, an undue influence over the representatives, and the improper means of fettering, embarrassing, or controuling the president or executive, we give the government, in the very out set, a fatal and pernicious tendency to that middle undesirable point—aristocracy. When we, as a circumstance not well to be avoided, admit the senate to a share of power in making treaties, and in managing foreign concerns, we certainly progress full far enough toward this most undesirable point in government. For with this power, also, I believe, we must join that of appointing ambassadors, other foreign ministers, and consuls, being powers necessarily connected.—In every point of view, in which I can contemplate this subject, it appears extremely clear to me, that the senate ought not generally to be a council of appointment. The legislature, after the people, is the great fountain of power, and ought to be kept as pure and uncorrupt as possible, from the hankerings, biasses, and contagion of offices—then the streams issuing from it, will be less tainted with those evils. It is not merely the number of impeachments, that are to be expected to make public officers honest and attentive in their business. A general opinion must pervade the community, that the house, the body to impeach them for misconduct, is disinterested, and ever watchful for the public good; and that the judges who shall try impeachments, will not feel a shadow of biass. Under such circumstances, men will not dare transgress, who, not deterred by such accusers and judges, would repeatedly misbehave. We have already suffered many and extensive evils, owing to the defects of the confederation, in not providing against the misconduct of public officers. When we expect the law to be punctually executed, not one man in ten thousand will disobey it: it is the probable chance of escaping punishment that induces men to transgress. It is one important mean to make the government just and honest, rigidly and constantly to hold, before the eyes of those who execute it, punishment, and dismission from office, for misconduct. These are principles no candid man, who has just ideas of the essential features of a free government, will controvert. They are, to be sure, at this period, called visionary, speculative, and anti-governmental—but in the true stile of courtiers, selfish politicians, and flatterers of despotism—discerning republican men of both parties see their value. They are said to be of no value, by empty boasting advocates for the constitution, who, by their weakness and conduct, in fact, injure its cause much more than most of its opponents. From their high sounding promises, men are led to expect a defence of it, and to have their doubts removed. When a number of long pieces appear, they, instead of the defence, &c. they expected, see nothing but a parade of names—volumes written without ever coming to the point— cases quoted between which and ours there is not the least similitude—and partial extracts made from histories and governments, merely to serve a purpose. Some of them, like the true admirers of royal and senatorial robes, would fain prove, that nations who have thought like freemen and philosophers about government, and endeavoured to be free, have often been the most miserable: if a single riot, in the course of five hundred years happened in a free country, if a salary, or the interest of a public or private debt was not paid at the moment, they seem to lay more stress upon these triffles (for triffles they are in a free and happy country) than upon the oppressions of despotic government for ages together. As to the lengthy writer in New-York you mention,* I have attentively examined his pieces; he appears to be a candid good-hearted man, to have a good stile, and some plausible ideas; but when we carefully examine his pieces, to see where the strength of them lies; when the mind endeavours to fix on those material parts, which ought to be the essence of all voluminous productions, we do not find them: the writer appears constantly to move on a smooth surface, the part of his work, like the parts of a cob-house, are all equally strong and all equally weak, and all like those works of the boys, without an object; his pieces appear to have but little relation to the great question, whether the constitution is fitted to the condition and character of this people or not. But to return— 3. Officers may be appointed by the president and an executive council—when we have assigned to the legislature the appointment of a few important officers—to the president and senate the appointment of those concerned in managing foreign affairs—to the state governments the appointment of militia officers, and authorise the legislature, by legislative acts, to assign to the president alone, to the heads of the departments, and courts of law respectively, the appointment of many inferior officers; we shall then want to lodge some where a residuum of power, a power to appoint all other necessary officers, as established by law. The fittest receptacle for this residuary power is clearly, in my opinion, the first executive magistrate, advised and directed by an executive council of seven or nine members, periodically chosen from such proportional districts as the union may for the

*A possible reference to *The Federalist* essays by Alexander Hamilton, James Madison, and John Jay.—Ed.

purpose be divided into. The people may give their votes for twice the number of counsellers wanted, and the federal legislature take twice the number also from the highest candidates, and from among them chuse the seven or nine, or number wanted. Such a council may be rationally formed for the business of appointments; whereas the senate, created for other purposes, never can be—Such councils form a feature in some of the best executives in the union—they appear to be essential to every first magistrate, who may frequently want advice.

To authorise the president to appoint his own council would he unsafe: to give the sole appointment of it to the legislature, would confer an undue and unnecessary influence upon that branch. Such a council for a year would be less expensive than the senate for four months. The president may nominate, and the counsellers always be made responsible for their advice and opinions, by recording and signing whatever they advise to be done. They and the president, to many purposes, will properly form an independent executive branch; have an influence unmixed with the legislative, which the executive never can have while connected with a powerful branch of the legislature. And yet the influence arising from the power of appointments be less dangerous, because in less dangerous hands—hands properly adequate to possess it. Whereas the senate, from its character and situation, will add a dangerous weight to the power itself, and be far less capable of responsibility, than the council proposed. There is another advantage; the residuum of power, as to appointments, which the president and council need possess, is less than that the president and senate must have. And as such a council would render the sessions of the senate unnecessary many months in the year, the expences of the government would not be increased, if they would not be lessened by the institution of such a council. I think I need not dwell upon this article, as the fitness of this mode of appointment will perhaps amply appear by the evident unfitness of the others.

4. Officers may be appointed by the president alone. It has been almost universally found, when a man has been authorized to exercise power alone, he has never done it alone; but, generally, aided his determinations by, and rested on the advice and opinions of others. And it often happens when advice is wanted, the worst men, the most interested creatures, the worst advice is at hand, obtrude themselves, and misdirect the mind of him who would be informed and advised. It is very seldom we see a single executive depend on accidental advice and assistance; but each single executive has, almost always, formed to itself a regular council, to be assembled and consulted on important occasions; this proves that a select council, of some kind, is, by experience, generally found necessary and useful. But in a free country, the exercise of any considerable branch of power ought to be under some checks and controuls. As to this point, I think the constitution stands well, the legislature may, when it shall deem it expedient, from time to time, authorise the president alone to appoint particular inferior officers, and when

necessary to take back the power. His power, therefore, in this respect, may always be increased or decreased by the legislature, as experience, the best instructor, shall direct: always keeping him, by the constitution, within certain bounds.

The FEDERAL FARMER.

XIV

The Executive Branch II

JANUARY 17, 1788.

DEAR SIR,

TO continue the subject of appointments:—Officers, in the fifth place, may be appointed by the heads of departments or courts of law. Art. 2. sect. 2. respecting appointments, goes on.—"But congress may by law vest the appointment of such inferior officers as they think proper in the president alone, in the courts of law, or in the heads of departments." The probability is, as the constitution now stands, that the senate, a branch of the legislature, will be tenacious of the power of appointment, and much too sparingly part with a share of it to the courts of law, and heads of departments. Here again the impropriety appears of the senate's having, generally, a share in the appointment of officers. We may fairly presume, that the judges, and principal officers in the departments, will be able well informed men in their respective branches of business; that they will, from experience, be best informed as to proper persons to fill inferior offices in them; that they will feel themselves responsible for the execution of their several branches of business, and for the conduct of the officers they may appoint therein.— From these, and other considerations, I think we may infer, that impartial and judicious appointments of subordinate officers will, generally, be made by the courts of law, and the heads of departments. This power of distributing appointments, as circumstances may require, into several hands, in a well formed disinterested legislature, might be of essential service, not only in promoting beneficial appointments, but, also, in preserving the balance in government: a feeble executive may be strengthened and supported by placing in its hands more numerous appointments; an executive too influential may be reduced within proper bounds, by placing many of the inferior appointments in the courts of law, and heads of departments; nor is there much danger that the executive will be wantonly weakened or strengthened by the legislature, by thus shifting the appointments of inferior officers, since all must be done by legislative acts which cannot be passed without the consent of the executive, or the consent of two-thirds of both branches—a good legislature will use this power to preserve the balance and perpetuate the government. Here again we are brought to our ultimatum:—is the legislature so constructed as to deserve our confidence?

6. Officers may be appointed by the state governments. By art. 1. sect. 8. the respective states are authorised exclusively to appoint the militia-officers. This not only lodges the appointments in proper places, but it also tends to distribute and lodge in different executive hands the powers of appointing to offices, so dangerous when collected into the hands of one or a few men.

It is a good general rule, that the legislative, executive, and judicial powers, ought to be kept distinct; but this, like other general rules, has its exceptions; and without these exceptions we cannot form a good government, and properly balance its parts: and we can determine only from reason, experience, and a critical inspection of the parts of the government, how far it is proper to intermix those powers. Appointments, I believe, in all mixed governments, have been assigned to different hands—some are made by the executive, some by the legislature, some by the judges, and some by the people. It has been thought adviseable by the wisest nations that the legislature should so far exercise executive and judicial powers as to appoint some officers judge of the elections of its members, and impeach and try officers for misconduct—that the executive should have a partial share in legislation—that judges should appoint some subordinate officers, and regulate so far as to establish rules for their own proceedings. Where the members of the government, as the house, the senate, the executive, and judiciary, are strong and complete, each in itself, the balance is naturally produced, each party may take the powers congenial to it, and we have less need to be anxious about checks, and the subdivision of powers.

If after making the deductions, already alluded to, from the general power to appoint federal officers the residuum shall be thought to be too large and unsafe, and to place an undue influence in the hands of the president and council, a further deduction may be made, with many advantages, and, perhaps, with but a few inconveniencies; and that is, by giving the appointment of a few great officers to the legislature—as of the commissioners of the treasury—of the comptroller, treasurer, master coiner, and some of the principal officers in the money department—of the sheriffs or marshalls of the United States—of states attornies, secretary of the home department, and secretary at war, perhaps, of the judges of the supreme court—of major-generals and admirals. The appointments of these officers, who may be at the heads of the great departments of business, in carrying into execution the national system, involve in them a variety of considerations; they will not often occur, and the power to make them ought to remain in safe hands. Officers of the above description are appointed by the legislatures in some of the states, and in some not. We may, I believe, presume that the federal legislature will possess sufficient knowledge and discernment to make judicious appointments: however, as these appointments by the legislature tend to increase a mixture of power, to lessen the advantages of impeachments and responsibility, I would by no means contend for them any further than it may be necessary for reducing the power of the executive within the bounds of safety. To determine with propriety, how extensive power the executive ought to possess relative to appointments, we must also examine the forms of it, and its other powers; and these forms and other powers I shall now proceed briefly to examine.

By art. 2. sect. 1. the executive power shall be vested in a president elected for four years, by electors to be appointed from time to time, in such manner as the state legislatures shall direct—the electors to be equal in numbers to the federal senators and representatives: but congress may determine the time of chusing senators, and the day on which they shall give their votes; and if no president be chosen by the electors, by a majority of votes, the states, as states in congress, shall elect one of the five highest on the list for president. It is to be observed, that in chusing the president, the principle of electing by a majority of votes is adopted; in chusing the vice-president, that of electing by a plurality. Viewing the principles and checks established in the election of the president, and especially considering the several states may guard the appointment of the electors as they shall judge best, I confess there appears to be a judicious combination of principles and precautions. Were the electors more numerous than they will be, in case the representation be not increased, I think, the system would be improved; not that I consider the democratic character so important in the choice of the electors as in the choice of representatives: be the electors more or less democratic, the president will be one of the very few of the most elevated characters. But there is danger, that a majority of a small number of electors may be corrupted and influenced, after appointed electors, and before they give their votes, especially if a considerable space of time elapse between the appointment and voting. I have already considered the advisory council in the executive branch: there are two things further in the organization of the executive to which I would particularly draw your attention; the first, which, is a single executive, I confess, I approve; the second, by which any person from period to period may be re-elected president, I think very exceptionable.

Each state in the union has uniformly shewn its preference for a single executive, and generally directed the first executive magistrate to act in certain cases by the advice of an executive council. Reason, and the experience of enlightened nations, seem justly to assign the business of making laws to numerous assemblies; and the execution of them, principally to the direction and care of one man. Independent of practice, a single man seems to be peculiarly well circumstanced to superintend the execution of laws with discernment and decision, with promptitude and unformity: the people usually point out a first man—he is to be seen in civilized as well as uncivilized nations—in republics as well as in other governments. In every large collection of people there must be a visible point serving as a common centre in the government, towards which to draw their eyes and attachments. The constitution must fix a man, or a congress of men, superior in the opinion of the people to the most popular men in the different parts of the community, else the people will be apt to divide and follow their respective leaders. Aspiring men, armies and navies, have not often been kept in tolerable order by the decrees of a senate or an executive council. The advocates for lodging the executive power in the hands of a number of equals, as an executive council, say, that much wisdom may be collected in such a council, and that it will be safe; but they agree, that it cannot be so prompt and responsible as a single man—they admit that such a council will generally consist of the aristocracy, and not stand so indifferent between it and the people as a first magistrate. But the principal objection made to a single man is, that when possessed of power he will be constantly struggling for more, disturbing the government, and encroaching on the rights of others. It must be admitted, that men, from the monarch down to the porter, are constantly aiming at power and importance and this propensity must be as constantly guarded against in the forms of the government. Adequate powers must be delegated to those who govern, and our security must be in limiting, defining, and guarding the exercise of them, so that those given shall not be abused, or made use of for openly or secretly seizing more. Why do we believe this abuse of power peculiar to a first magistrate? Is it because in the wars and contests of men, one man has often established his power over the rest? Or are men naturally fond of accumulating powers in the hands of one man? I do not see any similitude between the cases of those tyrants, who have sprung up in the midst of wars and tumults, and the cases of limited executives in established governments; nor shall we, on a careful examination, discover much likeness between the executives in Sweden, Denmark, Holland, &c. which have, from time to time, increased their powers, and become more absolute, and the executives, whose powers are well ascertained and defined, and which remain, by the constitution, only for a short and limited period in the hands of any one man or family. A single man, or family, can long and effectually direct its exertions to one point. There may be many favourable opportunities in the course of a man's life to seize on additional powers, and many more where powers are hereditary; and there are many circumstances favourable to usurpations, where the powers of the man or family are undefined, and such as often may be unduly extended before the people discover it. If we examine history attentively, we shall find that such exertions, such opportunities, and such circumstances as these have attended all the executives which have usurped upon the rights of the people, and which appear originally to have been, in some degree, limited. Admitting that moderate and even well defined powers, long in the hands of the same man or family, will, probably, be unreasonably increased, it will not follow that even extensive powers placed in the hands of a man only for a few years will be abused. The Roman consuls and Carthagenian suffetes possessed extensive powers while in office; but being annually appointed, they but seldom, if ever, abused them. The Roman dictators often possessed absolute power while in office; but usually being elected for short periods of time, no one of them for ages usurped upon the rights of the people. The kings of France, Spain, Sweden, Denmark, &c. have become absolute merely from the encroachments and abuse of power made by the nobles. As to kings, and limited monarchs, generally, history furnishes many more instances in which their powers have been abridged or annihilated by the nobles or people, or both, than in which they have been increased or made absolute; and in almost all the latter cases, we find the people were inattentive and fickle, and evidently were not born to be free. I am the more particular respecting this subject, because I have heard many mistaken observations relative to it. Men of property, and even men who hold powers for themselves and posterity, have too much to lose, wantonly to hazard a shock of the political system; the game must be large, and the chance of winning great, to induce them to risque what they have, for the uncertain prospect of gaining more. Our executive may be altogether elective, and possess no power, but as the substitute of the people, and that well limited, and only for a limited time. The great object is, in a republican government, to guard effectually against perpetuating any portion of power, great or small, in the same man or family; this perpetuation of power is totally uncongenial to the true spirit of republican governments: on the one hand the first executive magistrate ought to remain in office so long as to avoid instability in the execution of the laws; on the other, not so long as to enable him to take any measures to establish himself. The convention, it seems, first agreed that the president should be chosen for seven years, and never after to be eligible. Whether seven years is a period too long or not, is rather matter of opinion; but clear it is, that this mode is infinitely preferable to the one finally adopted. When a man shall get the chair, who may be re-elected, from time to time, for life, his greatest object will be to keep it; to gain friends and votes, at any rate; to associate some favourite son with himself, to take the office after him: whenever he shall have any prospect of continuing the office in himself and family, he will spare no artifice, no address, and no exertions, to increase the powers and importance of it; the servile supporters of his wishes will be placed in all offices, and tools constantly employed to aid his views and sound his praise. A man so situated will have no permanent interest in the government to lose, by contests and convulsions in the state, but always much to gain, and frequently the seducing and flattering hope of succeeding. If we reason at all on the subject, we must irresistably conclude, that this will be the case with nine tenths of the presidents; we may have, for the first president, and, perhaps, one in a century or two afterwards (if the government should withstand the attacks of others) a great and good man, governed by superior motives; but these are not events to be calculated upon in the present state of human nature.

A man chosen to this important office for a limited period, and always afterwards rendered, by the constitution, ineligible, will be governed by very different considerations: he can have no rational hopes or expectations of retaining his office after the expiration of a known limited time, or of continuing the office in his family, as by the constitution there must be a constant transfer of it from one man to another, and consequently from one family to another. No man will wish to be a mere cypher at the head of the government: the great object of each president then will be, to render his government a glorious period in the annals of his country. When a man constitutionally retires from office, he retires without pain; he is sensible he retires because the laws direct it, and not from the success of his rivals, nor with that public disapprobation which being left out, when eligible, implies. It is said, that a man knowing that at a given period he must quit his office, will unjustly attempt to take from the public, and lay in store the means of support and splendour in his retirement; there can, I think, be but very little in this observation. The same constitution that makes a man eligible for a given period only, ought to make no man eligible till he arrive to the age of forty or forty-five years; if he be a man of fortune, he will retire with dignity to his estate; if not, he may, like the Roman consuls, and other eminent characters in republics, find an honorable support and employment in some respectable office. A man who must, at all events, thus leave his office, will have but few or no temptations to fill its dependant offices with his tools, or any particular set of men; whereas the man constantly looking forward to his future elections, and, perhaps, to the aggrandizement of his family, will have every inducement before him to fill all places with his own props and dependants. As to public monies, the president need handle none of them, and he may always rigidly be made account for every shilling he shall receive.

On the whole, it would be, in my opinion, almost as well to create a limited monarchy at once, and give some family permanent power and interest in the community, and let it have something valuable to itself to lose in convulsions in the state, and in attempts of usurpation, as to make a first magistrate eligible for life, and to create hopes and expectations in him and his family, of obtaining what they have not. In the latter case, we actually tempt them to disturb the state, to foment struggles and contests, by laying before them the flattering prospect of gaining much in them without risking any thing.

The constitution provides only that the president shall hold his office during the term of four years; that, at most, only implies, that one shall be chosen every fourth year; it also provides, that in case of the removal, death, resignation, or inability, both of the president and vice-president, congress may declare what officer shall act as president; and that such officers shall act accordingly, until the disability be removed, *or a president shall be elected*: it also provides that congress may determine the time of chusing electors, and the day on which they shall give their votes. Considering these clauses together, I submit this question—whether in case of a vacancy in the office of president, by the removal, death, resignation, or inability of the president and vice-president, and congress should declare, that a certain officer, as secretary for foreign affairs, for instance, shall act as president, and suffer such officer to continue several years, or even for his life, to act as president, by omitting to appoint the time for chusing electors of another president, it would be any breach of the constitution? This appears to me to be an intended provision for supplying the office of president, not only for any remaining portion of the four years, but in cases of emergency, until another president shall be elected; and that at a period beyond the expiration of the four years: we do not know that it is impossible; we do not know that it is improbable, in case a popular officer should thus be declared the acting president, but that he might continue for life, and without any violent act, but merely by neglects and delays on the part of congress.

I shall conclude my observations on the organization of the legislature and executive, with making some remarks, rather as a matter of amusement, on the branch, or partial negative, in the legislation:—The third branch in the legislature may answer three valuable purposes, to impede in their passage hasty and intemperate laws, occasionally to assist the senate or people, and to prevent the legislature from encroaching upon the executive or judiciary. In Great-Britain the king has a complete negative upon all laws, but he very seldom exercises it. This may be well lodged in him, who possesses strength to support it, and whose family has independent and hereditary interests and powers, rights and prerogatives, in the government, to defend: but in a country where the first executive officer is elective, and has no rights, but in common with the people, a partial negative in legislation, as in Massachusetts and New-York, is, in my opinion, clearly best: in the former state, as before observed, it is lodged in the governor alone; in the latter, in the governor, chancellor, and judges of the supreme court—the new constitution lodges it in the president. This is simply a branch of legislative power, and has in itself no relation to executive or judicial powers. The question is, in what hands ought it to be lodged, to answer the three purposes mentioned the most advantageously? The prevailing opinion seems to be in favour of vesting it in the hands of the first executive magistrate. I will not say this opinion is ill founded. The negative, in one case, is intended to prevent hasty laws, not supported and revised by two-thirds of each of the two branches; in the second, it is to aid the weaker branch; and in the third, to defend the executive and judiciary. To answer these ends, there ought, therefore, to be collected in the hands which hold this negative, firmness, wisdom, and strength; the very object of the negative is occasional opposition to the two branches. By lodging it in the executive magistrate, we give him a share in making the laws, which he must execute; by associating the judges with him, as in New-York, we give them a share in making the laws, upon which they must decide as judicial magistrates; this may be a reason for excluding the judges: however, the negative in New-York is certainly well calculated to answer its great purposes: the governor and judges united must possess more firmness and strength, more wisdom and information, than either alone, and also more of the confidence of the people; and as to the balance among the departments, why should the executive alone hold the scales, and the judicial be left defenceless? I think the negative in New-York is found best in practice; we see it there frequently and wisely put upon the measures of the two branches; whereas in Massachusetts it is hardly ever exercised, and the governor, I believe, has often permitted laws to pass to which he had substantial objections, but did not make them; he, however, it is to be observed, is annually elected.

The FEDERAL FARMER.

XV

The Judiciary

JANUARY 18, 1788.

DEAR SIR,

BEFORE I proceed to examine particularly the powers vested, or which ought to be vested, in each branch of the proposed government, I shall briefly examine the organization of the remaining branch, the judicial, referring the particular examining of its powers to some future letters.

In forming this branch, our objects are—a fair and open, a wise and impartial interpretation of the laws—a prompt and impartial administration of justice, between the public and individuals, and between man and man. I believe, there is no feature in a free government more difficult to be well formed than this, especially in an extensive country, where the courts must be numerous, or the citizens travel to obtain justice.

The confederation impowers congress to institute judicial courts in four cases. 1. For settling disputes between individual states. 2. For determining, finally, appeals in all cases of captures. 3. For the trial of piracies and felonies committed on the high seas: And, 4. For the administration of martial law in the army and navy. The state courts in all other cases possess the judicial powers, in all questions arising on the laws of nations, of the union, and of the states individually—nor does congress appear to have any controul over state courts, judges or officers. The business of the judicial department is, properly speaking, judicial in part, in part executive, done by judges and juries, by certain recording and executive officers, as clerks, sheriffs, &c. they are all properly limbs, or parts, of the judicial courts, and have it in charge, faithfully to decide upon, and execute the laws, in judicial cases, between the public and individuals, between man and man. The recording and executive officers in this department, may well enough be formed by legislative acts, from time to time: but the offices, the situation, the powers and duties of judges and juries, are too important, as they respect the political system, as well as the administration of justice, not to be fixed on general principles by the constitution. It is true, the laws are made by the legislature; but the judges and juries, in their interpretations, and in directing the execution of them, have a very extensive influence for preserving or destroying liberty, and for changing the nature of the government. It is an observation of an approved writer, that judicial power is of such a nature, that when we have ascertained and fixed its limits, with all the caution and precision we can, it will yet be formidable, somewhat arbitrary and despotic—that is, after all our cares, we must leave a vast deal to the discretion and interpretation—to the wisdom, integrity, and politics of the judges—These men, such is the state even of the best laws, may do wrong, perhaps, in a thousand cases, sometimes with, and sometimes without design, yet it may be impracticable to convict them of misconduct. These considerations shew, how cautious a free people ought to be in forming this, as well as the other branches of their government, especially when connected with other considerations equally deserving of notice and attention. When the legislature makes a bad law, or the first executive magistrate usurps upon the rights of the people, they discover the evil much sooner, than the abuses of power in the judicial department; the proceedings of which are far more intricate, complex, and out of their immediate view. A bad law immediately excites a general alarm; a bad judicial determination, though not less pernicious in its consequences, is immediately felt, probably, by a single individual only, and noticed only by his neighbours, and a few spectators in the court. In this country, we have been always jealous of the legislature, and especially the executive; but not always of the judiciary: but very few men attentively consider the essential parts of it, and its proceedings, as they tend to support or to destroy free government: only a few professional men are in a situation properly to do this; and it is often alledged, that instances have not frequently occurred, in which they have been found very alert watchmen in the cause of liberty, or in the cause of democratic republics. Add to these considerations, that particular circumstances exist at this time to increase our inattention to limiting properly the judicial powers, we may fairly conclude, we are more in danger of sowing the seeds of arbitrary government in this department than in any other. In the unsettled state of things in this country, for several years past, it has been thought, that our popular legislatures have, sometimes, departed from the line of strict justice, while the law courts have shewn a disposition more punctually to keep to it. We are not sufficiently attentive to the circumstances, that the measures of popular legislatures naturally settle down in time, and gradually approach a mild and just medium; while the rigid systems of the law courts naturally become more severe and arbitrary, if not carefully tempered and guarded by the constitution, and by laws, from time to time. It is true, much has been written and said about some of these courts lately, in some of the states; but all has been about their fees, &c. and but very little to the purposes, as to their influence upon the freedom of the government.

By art. 3. sect. 1. the judicial power of the United States shall be vested in one supreme court, and in such inferior courts, as congress may, from time to time, ordain and establish—the judges of them to hold their offices during good behaviour, and to receive, at stated times, a compensation for their services, which shall not be diminished during their continuance in office; but which, I conceive, may be increased. By the same art. sect. 2. the supreme court shall have original jurisdiction, "in all cases affecting ambassadors, and other public ministers, and consuls, and those in which a state shall be a party, and appellate jurisdiction, *both as to law and fact,* in all other federal causes, with such exceptions, and under such regulations, as the congress shall make." By the same section, the judicial power shall extend in law and equity to all the federal cases therein enumerated. By the same section the jury trial, in criminal causes, except in cases of impeachment, is established; but not in civil causes, and the whole state may be considered as the vicinage in cases of crimes. These clauses present to view the constitutional features of the federal judiciary: this has been called a monster by some of the opponents, and some, even of the able advocates, have confessed they do not comprehend it. For myself, I confess, I see some good things in it, and some very extraordinary ones. "There shall be one supreme court." There ought in every government to be one court, in which all great questions in law shall finally meet and be determined: in Great-Britain, this is the house of lords, aided by all the superior judges; in Massachusetts, it is, at present, the supreme judicial court, consisting of five judges; in New-York, by the constitution, it is a court consisting of the president of the senate, the senators, chancellor and judges of the supreme court; and in the United States the federal supreme court, or this court in the last resort, may, by the legislature, be made to consist of three, five, fifty, or any other number of judges. The inferior federal courts are left by the constitution to be instituted and regulated altogether as the legislature shall judge best; and it is well provided, that the judges shall hold their offices during good behaviour. I shall not object to the line drawn between the original and appellate jurisdiction of the supreme court; though should we for safety, &c. be obliged to form a numerous supreme court, and place in it a considerable number of respectable characters, it will be found inconvenient for such a court, originally, to try all the causes affecting ambassadors, consuls, &c. Appeals may be carried up to the supreme court, under such regulations as congress shall make. Thus far the legislature does not appear to be limited to improper rules or principles in instituting judicial courts: indeed the legislature will have full power to form and arrange judicial courts in the federal cases enumerated, at pleasure, with these eight exceptions only. 1. There can be but one supreme federal judicial court. 2. This must have jurisdiction as to law and fact in the appellate causes. 3. Original jurisdiction, when foreign ministers and the states are concerned. 4. The judges of the judicial courts must continue in office during good behaviour—and, 5. Their salaries cannot be diminished while in office. 6. There must be a jury trial in criminal causes. 7. The trial of crimes must be in the state where committed—and, 8. There must be two witnesses to convict of treason.

In all other respects Congress may organize the judicial department according to their discretion; the importance of this power, among others proposed by the legislature (perhaps necessarily) I shall consider hereafter. Though there must, by the constitution, be but one judicial court, in which all the rays of judicial powers as to law, equity, and fact, in the cases enumerated must meet; yet this may be made by the legislature, a special court, consisting of any number of respectable characters or officers, the federal legislators excepted, to superintend the judicial department, to try the few causes in which foreign ministers and the states may be concerned, and to correct errors, as to law and fact, in certain important causes on appeals. Next below this judicial head, there may be several courts, such as are usually called superior courts, as a court of chancery, a court of criminal jurisdiction, a court of civil jurisdiction, a court of admiralty jurisdiction, a court of exchequer, &c. giving an appeal from these respectively to the supreme judicial court. These superior courts may be considered as so many points to which appeals may be brought up, from the various inferior courts, in the several branches of judicial causes. In all these superior and inferior courts, the trial by jury may be established in all cases, and the law and equity properly separated. In this organization, only a few very important causes, probably, would be carried up to the supreme court.— The superior courts would, finally, settle almost all causes. This organization, so far as it would respect questions of law, inferior, superior, and a special supreme court, would resemble that of New-York in a considerable degree, and those of several other states. This, I imagine, we must adopt, or else the Massachusetts plan; that is, a number of inferior courts, and one superior or supreme court, consisting of three, or five, or seven judges, in which one supreme court all the business shall be immediately collected from the inferior ones. The decision of the inferior courts, on either plan, probably will not much be relied on; and on the latter plan, there must be a prodigious accumulation of powers and business in all cases touching law, equity and facts, and all kinds of causes in a few hands, for whose errors of ignorance or design, there will be no possible remedy. As the legislature may adopt either of these, or any other plan, I shall not dwell longer on this subject.

In examining the federal judiciary, there appears to be some things very extraordinary and very peculiar. The judges or their friends may seize every opportunity to raise the judges salaries; but by the constitution they cannot be diminished. I am sensible how important it is that judges shall always have adequate and certain support; I am against their depending upon annual or periodical grants, because these may be withheld, or rendered too small by the dissent or narrowness of any one branch of the legislature; but there is a material distinction between periodical grants, and salaries held under permanent and standing laws: the former at stated periods cease, and must be renewed by the consent of all and every part of the legislature; the latter continue of course, and never will cease or be lowered, unless all parts of the legislature agree to do it. A man has as permanent an interest in his salary fixed by a standing law, so long as he may remain in office, as in any property he may possess; for the laws regulating the tenure of all property, are always liable to be altered by the legislature. The same judge may frequently be in office thirty or forty years; there may often be times, as in cases of war, or very high prices, when his salary may reasonably be increased one half or more; in a few years money may become scarce again, and prices fall, and his salary, with equal reason and propriety be decreased and lowered: not to suffer this to be done by consent of all the branches of the legislature, is, I believe, quite a novelty in the affairs of government. It is true, by a very forced and unnatural construction, the constitution of Massachusetts, by the governor and minority in the legislature, was made to speak this kind of language. Another circumstance ought to be considered; the mines which have been discovered are gradually exhausted, and the precious metals are continually wasting: hence the probability is, that money, the nominal representative of property, will gradually grow scarcer hereafter, and afford just reasons for gradually lowering salaries. The value of money depends altogether upon the quantity of it in circulation, which may be also decreased, as well as encreased, from a great variety of causes.

The supreme court, in cases of appeals, shall have jurisdiction both as to law and fact: that is in all civil causes carried up the supreme court by appeals, the court, or judges, shall try the fact and decide the law. Here an essential principle of the civil law is established, and the most noble and important principle of the common law exploded. To dwell a few minutes on this material point: the supreme court shall have jurisdiction both as to law and fact. What is meant by court? Is the jury included in the term, or is it not? I conceive it is not included: and so the members of convention, I am very sure, understand it. Court, or curia, was a term well understood long before juries existed; the people, and the best writers, in countries where there are no juries, uniformly use the word court, and can only mean by it the judge or judges who determine causes: also, in countries where there are juries we express ourselves in the same manner; we speak of the court of probate, court of chancery, justices court, alderman's court, &c. in which there is no jury. In our supreme courts, common pleas, &c. in which there are jury trials, we uniformly speak of the court and jury, and consider them as distinct. Were it necessary I might cite a multitude of cases from law books to confirm, beyond controversy, this position, that the jury is not included, or a part of the court.

But the supreme court is to have jurisdiction as to law and fact, under such regulations as congress shall make. I confess it is impossible to say how far congress may, with propriety, extend their regulations in this respect. I conceive, however, they cannot by any reasonable construction go so far as to admit the jury, on true common law principles, to try the fact, and give a general verdict. I have repeatedly examined this article: I think the meaning of it is, that the judges in all final questions, as to property and damages, shall have complete jurisdiction, to consider the whole cause, to examine the facts, and on a general view of them, and on principles of equity, as well as law, to give judgment.

As the trial by jury is provided for in criminal causes, I shall confine my observations to civil causes—and in these, I hold it is the established right of the jury by the common law, and the fundamental laws of this country, to give a general verdict in all cases when they chuse to do it, to decide both as to law and fact, whenever blended together in the issue put to them. Their right to determine as to facts will not be disputed, and their right to give a general verdict has never been disputed, except by a few judges and lawyers, governed by despotic principles. Coke, Hale, Holt, Blackstone, De Lome, and almost every other legal or political writer, who has written on the subject, has uniformly asserted this essential and important right of the jury. Juries in Great-Britain and America have universally practiced accordingly. Even Mansfield, with all his wishes about him, dare not directly avow the contrary. What fully confirms this point is, that there is no instance to be found, where a jury was ever punished for finding a general verdict, when a special one might, with propriety, have been found. The jury trial, especially politically considered, is by far the most important feature in the judicial department in a free country, and the right in question is far the most valuable part, and the last that ought to be yielded, of this trial. Juries are constantly and frequently drawn from the body of the people, and freemen of the country; and by holding the jury's right to return a general verdict in all cases sacred, we secure to the people at large, their just and rightful controul in the judicial department. If the conduct of judges shall be severe and arbitrary, and tend to subvert the laws, and change the forms of government, the jury may check them, by deciding against their opinions and determinations, in similar cases. It is true, the freemen of a country are not always minutely skilled in the laws, but they have common sense in its purity, which seldom or never errs in making and applying laws to the condition of the people, or in determining judicial causes, when stated to them by the parties. The body of the people, principally, bear the burdens of the community; they of right ought to have a controul in its important concerns, both in making and executing the laws, otherwise they may, in a short time, be ruined. Nor is it merely this controul alone we are to attend to; the jury trial brings with it an open and public discussion of all causes, and excludes secret and arbitrary proceedings. This, and the democratic branch in the legislature, as was formerly observed, are the means by which the people are let into the knowledge of public affairs— are enabled to stand as the guardians of each other's rights, and to restrain, by regular and legal measures, those who otherwise might infringe upon them. I am not unsupported in my opinion of the value of the trial by jury; not only British and American writers, but De Lome, and the most approved foreign writers, hold it to be the most valuable part of the British constitution, and indisputably the best mode of trial ever invented.

It was merely by the intrigues of the popish clergy, and of the Norman lawyers, that this mode of trial was not used in maritime, ecclesiastical, and military courts, and the civil law proceedings were introduced; and, I believe, it is more from custom and prejudice, than for any substantial reasons, that we do not in all the states establish the jury in our maritime as well as other courts.

In the civil law process the trial by jury is unknown; the consequence is, that a few judges and dependant officers, possess all the power in the judicial department. Instead of the open fair proceedings of the common law, where witnesses are examined in open court, and may be cross examined by the parties concerned—where council is allowed, &c. we see in the civil law process judges alone, who always, long previous to the trial, are known and often corrupted by ministerial influence, or by parties. Judges once influenced, soon become inclined to yield to temptations, and to decree for him who will pay the most for their partiality. It is, therefore, we find in the Roman, and almost all governments, where judges alone possess the judicial powers and try all cases, that bribery has prevailed. This, as well as the forms of the courts, naturally leads to secret and arbitrary proceedings—to taking evidence secretly—exparte, &c. to perplexing the cause—and to hasty decisions:—but, as to jurors, it is quite impracticable to bribe or influence them by any corrupt means; not only because they are untaught in such affairs, and possess the honest characters of the common freemen of a country; but because it is not, generally, known till the hour the cause comes on for trial, what persons are to form the jury.

But it is said, that no words could be found by which the states could agree to establish the jury trial in civil causes. I can hardly believe men to be serious, who make observations to this effect. The states have all derived judicial proceedings principally from one source, the British system; from the same common source the American lawyers have almost universally drawn their legal information. All the states have agreed to establish the trial by jury, in civil as well as in criminal causes. The several states, in congress, found no difficulty in establishing it in the Western Territory, in the ordinance passed in July 1787. We find, that the several states in congress, in establishing government in that territory, agreed, that the inhabitants of it, should always be entitled to the benefit of the trial by jury. Thus, in a few words, the jury trial is established in its full extent; and the convention with as much ease, have established the jury trial in criminal cases. In making a constitution, we are substantially to fix principles.—If in one state, damages on default are assessed by a jury, and in another by the judges—if in one state jurors are drawn out of a box, and in another not—if there be other trifling variations, they can be of no importance in the great question. Further, when we examine the prticular practices of the states, in little matters in judicial proceedings, I believe we shall find they differ near as much in criminal processes as in civil ones. Another thing worthy of notice in this place—the convention have used the word equity, and agreed to establish a chancery jurisdiction; about the meaning and extent of which, we all know, the several states disagree much more than about jury trials—in adopting the latter, they have very generally pursued the British plan; but as to the former, we see the states have varied, as their fears and opinions dictated.

By the common law, in Great-Britain and America, there is no appeal from the verdict of the jury, as to facts, to any judges whatever—the jurisdiction of the jury is complete and final in this; and only errors in law are carried up to the house of lords, the special supreme court in Great-Britain; or to the special supreme courts in Connecticut, New-York, New-Jersey, &c. Thus the juries are left masters as to facts; but, by the proposed constitution, directly the opposite principles is established. An appeal will lay in all appellate causes from the verdict of the jury, even as to mere facts, to the judges of the supreme court. Thus, in effect, we establish the civil law in this point; for if the jurisdiction of the jury be not final, as to facts, it is of little or no importance.

By art. 3. sect. 2. "the judicial power shall extend to all cases in law and equity, arising under this constitution, the laws of the United States," &c. What is here meant by equity? what is equity in a case arising under the constitution? possibly the clause might have the same meaning, were the words "in law and equity," omitted. Cases in law must differ widely from cases in law and equity. At first view, by thus joining the word equity with the word law, if we mean any thing, we seem to mean to give the judge a discretionary power. The word equity, in Great-Britain, has in time acquired a precise meaning—chancery proceedings there are now reduced to system—but this is not the case in the United States. In New-England, the judicial courts have no powers in cases in equity, except those dealt out to them by the legislature, in certain limited portions, by legislative acts. In New-York, Maryland, Virginia, and South-Carolina, powers to decide, in cases of equity, are vested in judges distinct from those who decide in matters of law: and the states generally seem to have carefully avoided giving unlimitedly, to the same judges, powers to decide in cases in law and equity. Perhaps, the clause would have the same meaning were the words, "this constitution," omitted: there is in it either a careless complex misuse of words, in themselves of extensive signification, or there is some meaning not easy to be comprehended. Suppose a case arising under the constitution—suppose the question judicially moved, whether, by the constitution, congress can suppress a state tax laid on polls, lands, or as an excise duty, which may be supposed to interfere with a federal tax. By the letter of the constitution, congress will appear to have no power to do it: but then the judges may decide the question on principles of equity as well as law. Now, omitting the words, "in law and equity," they may decide according to the spirit and true meaning of the constitution, as collected from what must appear to have been the intentions of the people when they made it. Therefore, it would seem, that if these words mean any thing, they must have a further meaning: yet I will not suppose it intended to lodge an arbitrary power or discretion in the judges, to decide as their conscience, their opinions, their caprice, or their politics might dictate. Without dwelling on this obscure clause, I will leave it to the examination of others.

The FEDERAL FARMER.

XVI

Arguments for a Bill of Rights

JANUARY 20, 1788.

DEAR SIR,

HAVING gone through with the organization of the government, I shall now proceed to examine more particularly those clauses which respect its powers. I shall begin with those articles and stipulations which are necessary for accurately ascertaining the extent of powers, and what is given, and for guarding, limiting, and restraining them in their exercise. We often find, these articles and stipulations placed in bills of rights; but they may as well be incorporated in the body of the constitution, as selected and placed by themselves. The constitution, or whole social compact, is but one instrument, no more or less, than a certain number of articles or stipulations agreed to by the people, whether it consists of articles, sections, chapters, bills of rights, or parts of any other denomination, cannot be material. Many needless observations, and idle distinctions, in my opinion, have been made respecting a bill of rights. On the one hand, it seems to be considered as a necessary distinct limb of the constitution, and as containing a certain number of very valuable articles, which are applicable to all societies: and, on the other, as useless, especially in a federal government, possessing only enumerated power—nay, dangerous, as individual rights are numerous, and not easy to be enumerated in a bill of rights, and from articles, or stipulations, securing some of them, it may be inferred, that others not mentioned are surrendered. There appears to me to be general indefinite propositions without much meaning—and the man who first advanced those of the latter description, in the present case, signed the federal constitution, which directly contradicts him. The supreme power is undoubtedly in the people, and it is a principle well established in my mind, that they reserve all powers not expressly delegated by them to those who govern; this is as true in forming a state as in forming a federal government. There is no possible distinction but this founded merely in the different modes of proceeding which take place in some cases. In forming a state constitution, under which to manage not only the great but the little concerns of a community: the powers to be possessed by the government are often too numerous to be enumerated; the people to adopt the shortest way often give general powers, indeed all powers, to the government, in some general words, and then, by a particular enumeration, take back, or rather say they however reserve certain rights as sacred, and which no laws shall be made to violate: hence the idea that all powers are given which are not reserved; but in forming a federal constitution, which *ex vi termine,* supposes state governments existing, and which is only to manage a few great national concerns, we often find it easier to enumerate particularly the powers to be delegated to the federal head, than to enumerate particularly the individual rights to be reserved; and the principle will operate in its full force, when we carefully adhere to it. When we particularly enumerate the powers given, we ought either carefully to enumerate the rights reserved, or be totally silent about them; we must either particularly enumerate both, or else suppose the particular enumeration of the powers given adequately draws the line between them and the rights reserved, particularly to enumerate the former and not the latter, I think most advisable; however, as men appear generally to have their doubts about these silent reservations, we might advantageously enumerate the powers given, and then in general words, according to the mode adopted in the 2d art. of the confederation, declare all powers, rights and privileges, are reserved, which are not explicitly and expressly given up. People, and very wisely too, like to be express and explicit about their essential rights, and not to be forced to claim them on the precarious and unascertained tenure of inferences and general principles, knowing that in any controversy between them and their rulers, concerning those rights, disputes may be endless, and nothing certain:—But admitting, on the general principle, that all rights are reserved of course, which are not expressly surrendered, the people could with sufficient certainty assert their rights on all occasions, and establish them with ease, still there are infinite advantages in particularly enumerating many of the most essential rights reserved in all cases; and as to the less important ones, we may declare in general terms, that all not expressly surrendered are reserved. We do not by declarations change the nature of things, or create new truths, but we give existence, or at least establish in the minds of the people truths and principles which they might never otherwise have thought of, or soon forgot. If a nation means its systems, religious or political, shall have duration, it ought to recognize the leading principles of them in the front page of every family book. What is the usefulness of a truth in theory, unless it exists constantly in the minds of the people, and has their assent:— we discern certain rights, as the freedom of the press, and the trial by jury, &c. which the people of England and of America of course believe to be sacred, and essential to their political happiness, and this belief in them is the result of ideas at first suggested to them by a few able men, and of subsequent experience; while the people of some other countries hear these rights mentioned with the utmost indifference; they think the privilege of existing at the will of a despot much preferable to them. Why this difference amongst beings every way formed alike. The reason of the difference is obvious—it is the effect of education, a series of notions impressed upon the minds of the people by examples, precepts and declarations. When the people of England got together, at the time they formed Magna Charta, they did not consider it sufficient, that they were indisputably entitled to certain natural and unalienable rights, not depending on silent titles, they, by a declaratory act, expressly recognized them, and explicitly declared to all the world, that they were entitled to enjoy those rights; they made an instrument in writing, and enumerated those they then thought essential, or in danger, and this wise men saw was not sufficient; and therefore, that the people might not forget these rights, and gradually become prepared for arbitrary government, their discerning and honest leaders caused this instrument to be confirmed near forty times, and to be read twice a year in public places, not that it would lose its validity without such confirmations, but to fix the contents of it in the minds of the people, as they successively come upon the stage.—Men, in some countries do not remain free, merely because they are entitled to natural and unalienable rights; men in all countries are entitled to them, not because their ancestors once got together and enumerated them on paper, but because, by repeated negotiations and declarations, all parties are brought to realize them, and of course to believe them to be sacred. Were it necessary, I might shew the wisdom of our past conduct, as a people, in not merely comforting ourselves that we were entitled to freedom, but in constantly keeping in view, in addresses, bills of rights, in news-papers, &c. the particular principles on which our freedom must always depend.

It is not merely in this point of view, that I urge the engrafting in the constitution additional declaratory articles. The distinction, in itself just, that all powers not given are reserved, is in effect destroyed by this very constitution, as I shall particularly demonstrate—and even independent of this, the people, by adopting the constitution, give many general undefined powers to congress, in the constitutional exercise of which, the rights in question may be affected. Gentlemen who oppose a federal bill of rights, or further declaratory articles, seem to view the subject in a very narrow imperfect manner. These have for their objects, not only the enumeration of the rights reserved, but principally to explain the general powers delegated in certain material points, and to restrain those who exercise them by fixed known boundaries. Many explanations and restrictions necessary and useful, would be much less so, were the people at large all well and fully acquainted with the principles and affairs of government. There appears to be in the constitution, a studied brevity, and it may also be probable, that several explanatory articles were omitted from a circumstance very common. What we have long and early understood ourselves in the common concerns of the community, we are apt to suppose is understood by others, and need not be expressed; and it is not unnatural or uncommon for the ablest men most frequently to make this mistake. To make declaratory articles unnecessary in an instrument of government, two circumstances must exist; the rights reserved must be indisputably so, and in their nature defined; the powers delegated to the government, must be precisely defined by the words that convey them, and clearly be of such extent and nature as that, by no reasonable construction, they can be made to invade the rights and prerogatives intended to be left in the people.

The first point urged, is, that all power is reserved not expressly given, that particular enumerated powers only are given, that all others are not given, but reserved, and that it is needless to attempt to restrain congress in the exercise of powers they possess not. This reasoning is logical, but of very little importance in the common affairs of men; but the constitution does not appear to respect it even in any view. To prove this, I might cite several clauses in it. I shall only remark on two or three. By article 1, section 9, "No title of nobility shall be granted by congress." Was this clause omitted, what power could congress have to make titles of nobility? In what part of the constitution would they find it? The answer must be, that congress would have no such power—that the people, by adopting the constitution, will not part with it. Why then by a negative clause, restrain congress from doing what it would have no power to do? This clause, then, must have no meaning, or imply, that were it omitted, congress would have the power in question, either upon the principle that some general words in the constitution may be so construed as to give it, or on the principle that congress possess the powers not expressly reserved. But this clause was in the confederation, and is said to be introduced into the constitution from very great caution. Even a cautionary provision implies a doubt, at least, that it is necessary; and if so in this case, clearly it is also alike necessary in all similar ones. The fact appears to be, that the people in forming the confederation, and the convention, in this instance, acted, naturally, they did not leave the point to be settled by general principles and logical inferences; but they settle the point in a few words, and all who read them at once understand them.

The trial by jury in criminal as well as in civil causes, has long been considered as one of our fundamental rights, and has been repeatedly recognized and confirmed by most of the state conventions. But the constitution expressly establishes this trial in criminal, and wholly omits it in civil causes. The jury trial in criminal causes, and the benefit of the writ of habeas corpus, are already as effectually established as any of the fundamental or essential rights of the people in the United States. This being the case, why in adopting a federal constitution do we now establish these, and omit all others, or all others, at least with a few exceptions, such as again agreeing there shall be no ex post facto laws, no titles of nobility, &c. We must consider this constitution, when adopted, as the supreme act of the people, and in construing it hereafter, we and our posterity must strictly adhere to the letter and spirit of it, and in no instance depart from them: in construing the federal constitution, it will be not only impracticable, but improper to refer to the state constitutions. They are entirely distinct instruments and inferior acts: besides, by the people's now establishing certain fundamental rights, it is strongly implied, that they are of opinion, that they would not otherwise be secured as a part of the federal system, or be regarded in the federal administration as fundamental. Further, these same rights, being established by the state constitutions, and secured to the people, our recognizing them now, implies, that the people thought them insecure by the state establishments, and extinguished or put afloat by the new arrangement of the social system, unless re-established.—Further, the people, thus establishing some few rights, and remaining totally silent about others similarly circumstanced, the implication indubitably is, that they mean to relinquish the latter, or at least feel indifferent about them. Rights, therefore, inferred from general principles of reason, being precarious and hardly ascertainable in the common affairs of society, and the people, in forming a federal constitution, explicitly shewing they conceive these rights to be thus circumstanced, and accordingly proceed to enumerate and establish some of them, the conclusion will be, that they have established all which they esteem valuable and sacred. On every principle, then, the people especially having began, ought to go through enumerating, and establish particularly all the rights of individuals, which can by any possibility come in question in making and executing federal laws. I have already observed upon the excellency and importance of the jury trial in civil as well as in criminal causes, instead of establishing it in criminal causes only; we ought to establish it generally;—instead of the clause of forty or fifty words relative to this subject, why not use the language that has always been used in this country, and say, "the people of the United States shall always be entitled to the trial by jury." This would shew the people still hold the right sacred, and enjoin it upon congress substantially to preserve the jury trial in all cases, according to the usage and custom of the country. I have observed before, that it is *the jury trial* we want; the little different appendages and modifications tacked to it in the different states, are no more than a drop in the ocean: the jury trial is a solid uniform feature in a free government; it is the substance we would save, not the little articles of form.

Security against ex post facto laws, the trial by jury, and the benefits of the writ of habeas corpus, are but a part of those inestimable rights the people of the United States are entitled to, even in judicial proceedings, by the course of the common law. These may be secured in general words, as in New-York, the Western Territory, &c. by declaring the people of the United States shall always be entitled to judicial proceedings according to the course of the common law, as used and established in the said states. Perhaps it would be better to enumerate the particular essential rights the people are entitled to in these proceedings, as has been done in many of the states, and as has been done in England. In this case, the people may proceed to declare, that no man shall be held to answer to any offence, till the same be fully described to him; nor to furnish evidence against himself: that, except in the government of the army and navy, no person shall be tried for any offence, whereby he may incur loss of life, or an infamous punishment, until he be first indicted by a grand jury; that every person shall have a right to produce all proofs that may be favourable to him, and to meet the witnesses against him face to face; that every person shall be entitled to obtain right and justice freely and without delay: that all persons shall have a right to be secure from all unreasonable searches and seizures of their persons, houses, papers, or possessions; and that all warrants shall be deemed contrary to this right, if the foundation of them be not previously supported by oath, and there be not in them a special designation of persons or objects of search, arrest, or seizure: and that no person shall be exiled or molested in his person or effects, otherwise than by the judgment of his peers, or according to the law of the land. A celebrated writer observes upon this last article, that in itself it may be said to comprehend the whole end of political society. These rights are not necessarily reserved, they are established, or enjoyed but in few countries: they are stipulated rights, almost peculiar to British and American laws. In the execution of those laws, individuals, by long custom, by magna charta, bills of rights &c. have become entitled to them. A man, at first, by act of parliament, became entitled to the benefits of the writ of habeas corpus—men are entitled to these rights and benefits in the judicial proceedings of our state courts generally: but it will by no means follow, that they will be entitled to them in the federal courts, and have a right to assert them, unless secured and established by the constitution or federal laws. We certainly, in federal processes, might as well claim the benefits of the writ of habeas corpus, as to claim trial by a jury—the right to have council—to have witnesses face to face—to be secure against unreasonable search warrants, &c. was the constitution silent as to the whole of them:—but the establishment of the former, will evince that we could not claim them without it; and the omission of the latter, implies they are relinquished, or deemed of no importance. These are rights and benefits individuals acquire by compact; they must claim them under compacts, or immemorial usage—it is doubtful, at least, whether they can be claimed under immemorial usage in this country; and it is, therefore, we generally claim them under compacts, as charters and constitutions.

The people by adopting the federal constitution, give congress general powers to institute a distinct and new judiciary, new courts, and to regulate all proceedings in them under the eight limitations mentioned in a former letter; and the further one, that the benefits of the habeas corpus act shall be enjoyed by individuals. Thus general powers being given to institute courts, and regulate their proceedings, with no provision for securing the rights principally in question, may not congress so exercise those powers, and constitutionally too, as to destroy those rights? clearly, in my opinion, they are not in any degree secured. But, admitting the case is only doubtful, would it not be prudent and wise to secure them and remove all doubts, since all agree the people ought to enjoy these valuable rights, a very few men excepted, who seem to be rather of opinion that there is little or nothing in them? Were it necessary I might add many observations to shew their value and political importance.

The constitution will give congress general powers to raise and support armies. General powers carry with them incidental ones, and the means necessary to the end. In the exercise of these powers, is there any provision in the constitution to prevent the quartering of soldiers on the inhabitants? you will answer, there is not. This may sometimes be deemed a necessary measure in the support of armies; on what principle can the people claim the right to be exempt from this burden? they will urge, perhaps, the practice of the country, and the provisions made in some of the state constitutions—they will be answered, that their claim thus to be exempt, is not founded in nature, but only in custom and opinion, or at best, in stipulations in some of the state constitutions, which are local, and inferior in their operation, and can have no controul over the general government—that they had adopted a federal constitution—had noticed several rights, but had been totally silent about this exemption—that they had given general powers relative to the subject, which, in their operation, regularly destroyed the claim. Though it is not to be presumed, that we are in any immediate danger from this quarter, yet it is fit and proper to establish, beyond dispute, those rights which are particularly valuable to individuals, and essential to the permanency and duration of free government. An excellent writer observes, that the English, always in possession of their freedom, are frequently unmindful of the value of it: we, at this period, do not seem to be so well off, having, in some instances abused ours; many of us are quite disposed to barter it away for what we call energy, coercion, and some other terms we use as vaguely as that of liberty—There is often as great a rage for change and novelty in politics, as in amusements and fashions.

All parties apparently agree, that the freedom of the press is a fundamental right, and ought not to be restrained by any taxes, duties, or in any manner whatever. Why should not the people, in adopting a federal constitution, declare this, even if there are only doubts about it. But, say the advocates, all powers not given are reserved:—true; but the great question is, are not powers given, in the exercise of which this right may be destroyed? The people's or the printers' claim to a free press, is founded on the fundamental laws, that is, compacts, and state constitutions, made by the people. The people, who can annihilate or alter those constitutions, can annihilate or limit this right. This may be done by giving general powers, as well as by using particular words. No right claimed under a state constitution, will avail against a law of the union, made in pursuance of the federal constitution: therefore the question is, what laws will congress have a right to make by the constitution of the union, and particularly touching the press? By art. 1. sect. 8. congress will have power to lay and collect taxes, duties, imposts and excise. By this congress will clearly have power to lay and collect all kinds of taxes whatever—taxes on houses, lands, polls, industry, merchandize, &c.— taxes on deeds, bonds, and all written instruments—on writs, pleas, and all judicial proceedings, on licences, naval officers' papers, &c. on newspapers, advertisements, &c. and to require bonds of the naval officers, clerks, printers, &c. to account for the taxes that may become due on papers that go through their hands. Printing, like all other business, must cease when taxed beyond its profits; and it appears to me, that a power to tax the press at discretion, is a power to destroy or restrain the freedom of it. There may be other powers given, in the exercise of which this freedom may be effected; and certainly it is of too much importance to be left thus liable to be taxed, and constantly to constructions and inferences. A free press is the channel of communication as to mercantile and public affairs; by means of it the people in large countries ascertain each others sentiments; are enabled to unite, and become formidable to those rulers who adopt improper measures. Newspapers may sometimes be the vehicles of abuse, and of many things not true; but these are but small inconveniencies, in my mind, among many advantages. A celebrated writer, I have several times quoted, speaking in high terms of the English liberties, says, "lastly the key stone was put to the arch, by the final establishment of the freedom of the press." I shall not dwell longer upon the fundamental rights, to some of which I have attended in this letter, for the same reasons that these I have mentioned, ought to be expressly secured, lest in the exercise of general powers given they may be invaded: it is pretty clear, that some other of less importance, or less in danger, might with propriety also be secured.

I shall now proceed to examine briefly the powers proposed to be vested in the several branches of the government, and especially the mode of laying and collecting internal taxes.

The FEDERAL FARMER.

XVII

Federal versus Consolidated Government

JANUARY 23, 1788.

DEAR SIR,

I BELIEVE the people of the United States are full in the opinion, that a free and mild government can be preserved in their extensive territories, only under the substantial forms of a federal republic. As several of the ablest advocates for the system proposed, have acknowledged this (and I hope the confessions they have published will be preserved and remembered) I shall not take up time to establish this point. A question then arises, how far that system partakes of a federal republic.—I observed in a former letter, that it appears to be the first important step to a consolidation of the states; that its strong tendency is to that point.

But what do we mean by a federal republic? and what by a consolidated government? To erect a federal republic, we must first make a number of states on republican principles; each state with a government organized for the internal management of its affairs: The states, as such, must unite under a federal head, and delegate to it powers to make and execute laws in certain enumerated cases, under certain restrictions; this head may be a single assembly, like the present congress, or the Amphictionic council; or it may consist of a legislature, with one or more branches; of an executive, and of a judiciary. To form a consolidated, or one entire government, there must be no state, or local governments, but all things, persons and property, must be subject to the laws of one legislature alone; to one executive, and one judiciary. Each state government, as the government of New-Jersey, &c. is a consolidated, or one entire government, as it respects the counties, towns, citizens and property within the limits of the state.—The state governments are the basis, the pillar on which the federal head is placed, and the whole together, when formed on elective principles, constitute a federal republic. A federal republic in itself supposes state or local governments to exist, as the body or props, on which the federal head rests, and that it cannot remain a moment after they cease. In erecting the federal government, and always in its councils, each state must be known as a sovereign body; but in erecting this government, I conceive, the legislature of the state, by the expressed or implied assent of the people, or the people of the state, under the direction of the government of it, may accede to the federal compact: Nor do I conceive it to be necessarily a part of a confederacy of states, that each have an equal voice in the general councils. A confederated republic being organized, each state must retain powers for managing its internal police, and all delegate to the union power to manage general concerns: The quantity of power the union must possess is one thing, the mode of exercising the powers given, is quite a different consideration; and it is the mode of exercising them, that makes one of the essential distinctions between one entire or consolidated government, and a federal republic; that is, however the government may be organized, if the laws of the union, in most important concerns, as in levying and collecting taxes, raising troops, &c. operate immediately upon the persons and property of individuals, and not on states, extend to organizing the militia, &c. the government, as to its administration, as to making and executing laws, is not federal, but consolidated. To illustrate my idea—the union makes a requisition, and assigns to each state its quota of men or monies wanted; each state, by its own laws and officers, in its own way, furnishes its quota: here the state governments stand between the union and individuals; the laws of the union operate only on states, as such, and federally: Here nothing can be done without the meetings of the state legislatures—but in the other case the union, though the state legislatures should not meet for years together, proceeds immediately, by its own laws and officers, to levy and collect monies of individuals, to inlist men, form armies, &c. here the laws of the union operate immediately on the body of the people, on persons and property; in the same manner the laws of one entire consolidated government operate.—These two modes are very distinct, and in their operation and consequences have directly opposite tendencies: The first makes the existence of the state governments indispensable, and throws all the detail business of levying and collecting the taxes, &c. into the hands of those governments, and into the hands, of course, of many thousand officers solely created by, and dependent on the state. The last entirely excludes the agency of the respective states, and throws the whole business of levying and collecting taxes, &c. into the hands of many thousand officers solely created by and dependent upon the union, and makes the existence of the state government of no consequence in the case. It is true, congress in raising any given sum in direct taxes, must by the constitution, raise so much of it in one state, and so much in another, by a fixed rule, which most of the states some time since agreed to: But this does not affect the principle in question, it only secures each state against any arbitrary proportions. The federal mode is perfectly safe and eligible, founded in the true spirit of a confederated republic, there could be no possible exception to it, did we not find by experience, that the states will sometimes neglect to comply with the reasonable requisitions of the union. It being according to the fundamental principles of federal republics, to raise men and monies by requisitions, and for the states individually to organize and train the militia, I conceive, there can be no reason whatever for departing from them, except this, that the states sometimes neglect to comply with reasonable requisitions, and that it is dangerous to attempt to compel a delinquent state by force, as it may often produce a war. We ought, therefore, to enquire attentively, how extensive the evils to be guarded against are, and cautiously limit the remedies to the extent of the evils. I am not about to defend the confederation, or to charge the proposed constitution with imperfections not in it; but we ought to examine facts, and strip them of the false colourings often given them by incautious observations, by unthinking or designing men. We ought to premise, that laws for raising men and monies, even in consolidated governments, are not often punctually complied with. Historians, except in extraordinary cases, but very seldom take notice of the detail collection of taxes; but these facts we have fully proved, and well attested; that the most energetic governments have relinquished taxes frequently, which were of many years standing. These facts amply prove, that taxes assessed, have remained many years uncollected. I agree there have been instances in the republics of Greece, Holland, &c. in the course of several centuries, of states neglecting to pay their quotas of requisitions; but it is a circumstance certainly deserving of attention, whether these nations which have depended on requisitions principally for their defence, have not raised men and monies nearly as punctually as entire governments, which have taxed directly; whether we have not found the latter as often distressed for the want of troops and monies as the former. It has been said, that the Amphictionic council, and the Germanic head, have not possessed sufficient powers to controul the members of the republic in a proper manner. Is this, if true, to be imputed to requisitions? Is it not principally to be imputed to the unequal powers of those members, connected with this important circumstance, that each member possessed power to league itself with foreign powers, and powerful neighbours, without the consent of the head. After all, has not the Germanic body a government as good as its neighbours in general? and did not the Grecian republic remain united several centuries, and form the theatre of human greatness? No government in Europe has commanded monies more plentifully than the government of Holland. As to the United States, the separate states lay taxes directly, and the union calls for taxes by way of requisitions; and is it a fact, that more monies are due in proportion on requisitions in the United States, than on the state taxes directly laid?—It is but about ten years since congress begun to make requisitions, and in that time, the monies, &c. required, and the bounties given for men required of the states, have amounted, specie value, to about 36 millions dollars, about 24 millions of dollars of which have been actually paid; and a very considerable part of the 12 millions not paid, remains so not so much from the neglect of the states, as from the sudden changes in paper money, &c. which in a great measure rendered payments of no service, and which often induced the union indirectly to relinquish one demand, by making another in a different form. Before we totally condemn requisitions, we ought to consider what immense bounties the states gave, and what prodigious exertions they made in the war, in order to comply with the requisitions of congress; and if since the peace they have been delinquent, ought we not carefully to enquire, whether that delinquency is to be imputed solely to the nature of requisitions? ought it not in part to be imputed to two other causes? I mean first, an opinion, that has extensively prevailed, that the requisitions for domestic interest have not been founded on just principles; and, secondly, the circumstance, that the government itself, by proposing imposts, &c. has departed virtually from the constitutional system; which proposed changes, like all changes proposed in government, produce an inattention and negligence in the execution of the government in being.

I am not for depending wholly on requisitions; but I mention these few facts to shew they are not so totally futile as many pretend. For the truth of many of these facts I appeal to the public records; and for the truth of the others, I appeal to many republican characters, who are best informed in the affairs of the United States. Since the peace, and till the convention reported, the wisest men in the United States generally supposed, that certain limited funds would answer the purposes of the union: and though the states are by no means in so good a condition as I wish they were, yet, I think, I may very safely affirm, they are in a better condition than they would be had congress always possessed the powers of taxation now contended for. The fact is admitted, that our federal government does not possess sufficient powers to give life and vigor to the political system; and that we experience disappointments, and several inconveniences; but we ought carefully to distinguish those which are merely the consequences of a severe and tedious war, from those which arise from defects in the federal system. There has been an entire revolution in the United States within thirteen years, and the least we can compute the waste of labour and property at, during that period, by the war, is three hundred million of dollars. Our people are like a man just recovering from a severe fit of sickness. It was the war that disturbed the course of commerce, introduced floods of paper money, the stagnation of credit, and threw many valuable men out of steady business. From these sources our greatest evils arise; men of knowledge and reflection must perceive it;—but then, have we not done more in three or four years past, in repairing the injuries of the war, by repairing houses and estates, restoring industry, frugality, the fisheries, manufactures, &c. and thereby laying the foundation of good government, and of individual and political happiness, than any people ever did in a like time; we must judge from a view of the country and facts, and not from foreign newspapers, or our own, which are printed chiefly in the commercial towns, where imprudent living, imprudent importations, and many unexpected disappointments, have produced a despondency, and a disposition to view every thing on the dark side. Some of the evils we feel, all will agree, ought to be imputed to the defective administration of the governments. From these and various considerations, I am very clearly of opinion, that the evils we sustain, merely on account of the defects of the confederation, are but as a feather in the balance against a mountain, compared with those which would, infallibly, be the result of the loss of general liberty, and that happiness men enjoy under a frugal, free, and mild government.

Heretofore we do not seem to have seen danger any where, but in giving power to congress, and now no where but in congress wanting powers; and, without examining the extent of the evils to be remedied, by one step, we are for giving up to congress almost all powers of any importance without limitation. The defects of the confederation are extravagantly magnified, and every species of pain we feel imputed to them: and hence it is inferred, there must be a total change of the principles, as well as forms of government: and in the main point, touching the federal powers, we rest all on a logical inference, totally inconsistent with experience and sound political reasoning.

It is said, that as the federal head must make peace and war, and provide for the common defence, it ought to possess all powers necessary to that end: that powers unlimited, as to the purse and sword, to raise men and monies, and form the militia, are necessary to that end; and, therefore, the federal head ought to possess them. This reasoning is far more specious than solid: it is necessary that these powers so exist in the body politic, as to be called into exercise whenever necessary for the public safety; but it is by no means true, that the man, or congress of men, whose duty it more immediately is to provide for the common defence, ought to possess them without limitation. But clear it is, that if such men, or congress, be not in a situation to hold them without danger to liberty, he or they ought not to possess them. It has long been thought to be a well founded position, that the purse and sword ought not to be placed in the same hands in a free government. Our wise ancestors have carefully separated them—placed the sword in the hands of their king, even under considerable limitations, and the purse in the hands of the commons alone: yet the king makes peace and war, and it is his duty to provide for the common defence of the nation. This authority at least goes thus far—that a nation, well versed in the science of government, does not conceive it to be necessary or expedient for the man entrusted with the common defence and general tranquility, to possess unlimitedly the powers in question, or even in any considerable degree. Could he, whose duty it is to defend the public, possess in himself independently, all the means of doing it consistent with the public good, it might be convenient: but the people of England know that their liberties and happiness would be in infinitely greater danger from the king's unlimited possession of these powers, than from all external enemies and internal commotions to which they might be exposed: therefore, though they have made it his duty to guard the empire, yet they have wisely placed in other hands, the hands of their representatives, the power to deal out and controul the means. In Holland their high mightinesses must provide for the common defence, but for the means they depend, in a considerable degree, upon requisitions made on the state or local assemblies. Reason and facts evince, that however convenient it might be for an executive magistrate, or federal head, more immediately charged with the national defence and safety, solely, directly, and independently to possess all the means; yet such magistrate, or head, never ought to possess them, if thereby the public liberties shall be endangered. The powers in question never have been, by nations wise and free, deposited, nor can they ever be, with safety, anywhere, but in the principal members of the national system;—where these form one entire government, as in Great-Britain, they are separated and lodged in the principal members of it. But in a federal republic, there is quite a different organization; the people form this kind of government, generally, because their territories are too extensive to admit of their assembling in one legislature, or of executing the laws on free principles under one entire government. They convene in their local assemblies, for local purposes, and for managing their internal concerns, and unite their states under a federal head for general purposes. It is the essential characteristic of a confederated republic, that this head be dependant on, and kept within limited bounds by, the local governments; and it is because, in these alone, in fact, the people can be substantially assembled or represented. It is, therefore, we very universally see, in this kind of government, the congressional powers placed in a few hands, and accordingly limited, and specifically enumerated: and the local assemblies strong and well guarded, and composed of numerous members. Wise men will always place the controuling power where the people are substantially collected by their representatives. By the proposed system, the federal head will possess, without limitation, almost every species of power that can, in its exercise, tend to change the government, or to endanger liberty; while in it, I think it has been fully shewn, the people will have but the shadow of representation, and but the shadow of security for their rights and liberties. In a confederated republic, the division of representation, &c. in its nature, requires a correspondent division and deposit of powers, relative to taxes and military concerns: and I think the plan offered stands quite alone, in confounding the principles of governments in themselves totally distinct. I wish not to exculpate the states for their improper neglects in not paying their quotas of requisitions; but, in applying the remedy, we must be governed by reason and facts. It will not be denied, that the people have a right to change the government when the majority chuse it, if not restrained by some existing compact—that they have a right to displace their rulers, and consequently to determine when their measures are reasonable or not—and that they have a right, at any time, to put a stop to those measures they may deem prejudicial to them, by such forms and negatives as they may see fit to provide. From all these, and many other well founded considerations, I need not mention, a question arises, what powers shall there be delegated to the federal head, to insure safety, as well as energy, in the government? I think there is a safe and proper medium pointed out by experience, by reason, and facts. When we have organized the government, we ought to give power to the union, so far only as experience and present circumstances shall direct, with a reasonable regard to time to come. Should future circumstances, contrary to our expectations, require that further powers be transferred to the union, we can do it far more easily, than get back those we may now imprudently give. The system proposed is untried: candid advocates and opposers admit, that it is, in a degree, a mere experiment, and that its organization is weak and imperfect; surely then, the safe ground is cautiously to vest power in it, and when we are sure we have given enough for ordinary exigencies, to be extremely careful how we delegate powers, which, in common cases, must necessarily be useless or abused, and of very uncertain effect in uncommon ones.

By giving the union power to regulate commerce, and to levy and collect taxes by imposts, we give it an extensive authority, and permanent productive funds, I believe quite as adequate to the present demands of the union, as exises and direct taxes can be made to the present demands of the separate states. The state governments are now about four times as expensive as that of the union; and their several state debts added together, are nearly as large as that of the union—Our impost duties since the peace have been almost as productive as the other sources of taxation, and when under one general system of regulations, the probability is, that those duties will be very considerably increased: Indeed the representation proposed will hardly justify giving to congress unlimited powers to raise taxes by imposts, in addition to the other powers the union must necessarily have. It is said, that if congress possess only authority to raise taxes by imposts, trade probably will be over-burdened with taxes, and the taxes of the union be found inadequate to any uncommon exigencies: To this we may observe, that trade generally finds its own level, and will naturally and necessarily heave off any undue burdens laid upon it: further, if congress alone possess the impost, and also unlimited power to raise monies by excises and direct taxes, there must be much more danger that two taxing powers, the union and states, will carry excises and direct taxes to an unreasonable extent, especially as these have not the natural boundaries taxes on trade have. However, it is not my object to propose to exclude congress from raising monies by internal taxes, as by duties, excises, and direct taxes; but my opinion is, that congress, especially in its proposed organization, ought not to raise monies by internal taxes, except in strict conformity to the federal plan; that is, by the agency of the state governments in all cases, except where a state shall neglect, for an unreasonable time, to pay its quota of a requisition; and never where so many of the state legislatures as represent a majority of the people, shall formally determine an excise law or requisition is improper, in their next session after the same be laid before them. We ought always to recollect that the evil to be guarded against is found by our own experience, and the experience of others, to be mere neglect in the states to pay their quotas; and power in the union to levy and collect the neglecting states' quotas with interest, is fully adequate to the evil. By this federal plan, with this exception mentioned, we secure the means of collecting the taxes by the usual process of law, and avoid the evil of attempting to compel or coerce a state; and we avoid also a circumstance, which never yet could be, and I am fully confident never can be, admitted in a free federal republic; I mean a permanent and continued system of tax laws of the union, executed in the bowels of the states by many thousand officers, dependent as to the assessing and collecting federal taxes, solely upon the union. On every principle then, we ought to provide, that the union render an exact account of all monies raised by imposts and other taxes; and that whenever monies shall be wanted for the purposes of the union, beyond the proceeds of the impost duties, requisitions shall be made on the states for the monies so wanted; and that the power of laying and collecting shall never be exercised, except in cases where a state shall neglect, a given time, to pay its quota. This mode seems to be strongly pointed out by the reason of the case, and spirit of the government; and I believe, there is no instance to be found in a federal republic, where the congressional powers ever extended generally to collecting monies by direct taxes or excises. Creating all these restrictions, still the powers of the union in matters of taxation, will be too unlimited; further checks, in my mind, are indispensably necessary. Nor do I conceive, that as full a representation as is practicable in the federal government, will afford sufficient security: the strength of the government, and the confidence of the people, must be collected principally in the local assemblies; every part or branch of the federal head must be feeble, and unsafely trusted with large powers. A government possessed of more power than its constituent parts will justify, will not only probably abuse it, but be unequal to bear its own burden; it may as soon be destroyed by the pressure of power, as languish and perish for want of it.

There are two ways further of raising checks, and guarding against undue combinations and influence in a federal system. The first is, in levying taxes, raising and keeping up armies, in building navies, in forming plans for the militia, and in appropriating monies for the support of the military, to require the attendance of a large proportion of the federal representatives, as two-thirds or three-fourths of them; and in passing laws, in these important cases, to require the consent of two-thirds or three-fourths of the members present. The second is, by requiring that certain important laws of the federal head, as a requisition or a law for raising monies by excise shall be laid before the state legislatures, and if disapproved of by a given number of them, say by as many of them as represent a majority of the people, the law shall have no effect. Whether it would be adviseable to adopt both, or either of these checks, I will not undertake to determine. We have seen them both exist in confederated republics. The first exists substantially in the confederation, and will exist in some measure in the plan proposed, as in chusing a president by the house, in expelling members; in the senate, in making treaties, and in deciding on impeachments, and in the whole in altering the constitution. The last exists in the United Netherlands, but in a much greater extent. The first is founded on this principle, that these important measures may, sometimes, be adopted by a bare quorum of members, perhaps, from a few states, and that a bare majority of the federal representatives may frequently be of the aristocracy, or some particular interests, connections, or parties in the community, and governed by motives, views, and inclinations not compatible with the general interest.—The last is founded on this principle, that the people will be substantially represented, only in their state or local assemblies; that their principal security must be found in them; and that, therefore, they ought to have ultimately a constitutional controul over such interesting measures.

I have often heard it observed, that our people are well informed, and will not submit to oppressive governments; that the state governments will be their ready advocates, and possess their confidence, mix with them, and enter into all their wants and feelings. This is all true; but of what avail will these circumstances be, if the state governments, thus allowed to be the guardians of the people, possess no kind of power by the forms of the social compact, to stop, in their passage, the laws of congress injurious to the people. State governments must stand and see the law take place; they may complain and petition—so may individuals; the members of them, in extreme cases, may resist, on the principles of self-defence—so may the people and individuals.

It has been observed, that the people, in extensive territories, have more power, compared with that of their rulers, than in small states. Is not directly the opposite true? The people in a small state can unite and act in concert, and with vigour; but in large territories, the men who govern find it more easy to unite, while people cannot; while they cannot collect the opinions of each part, while they move to different points, and one part is often played off against the other.

It has been asserted, that the confederate head of a republic at best, is in general weak and dependent:—that the people will attach themselves to, and support their local governments, in all disputes with the union. Admit the fact: is it any way to remove the inconvenience by accumulating powers upon a weak organization? The fact is, that the detail administration of affairs, in this mixed republic, depends principally on the local governments; and the people would be wretched without them: and a great proportion of social happiness depends on the internal administration of justice, and on internal police. The splendor of the monarch, and the power of the government are one thing. The happiness of the subject depends on very different causes; but it is to the latter, that the best men, the greatest ornaments of human nature, have most carefully attended: it is to the former tyrants and oppressors have always aimed.

The FEDERAL FARMER.

The Constitution's Provisions
for Distributing Powers
between the General and State
Governments

JANUARY 25, 1788.

DEAR SIR,

I AM persuaded, a federal head never was formed, that possessed half the powers which it could carry into full effect, altogether independently of the state or local governments, as the one, the convention has proposed, will possess. Should the state legislatures never meet, except merely for chusing federal senators and appointing electors, once in four and six years, the federal head may go on for ages to make all laws relative to the following subjects, and by its own courts, officers, and provisions, carry them into full effect, and to any extent it may deem for the general welfare; that is, for *raising taxes,* borrowing and coining monies, and for applying them—for forming and governing *armies* and *navies* and for directing their operations—for regulating commerce with foreign nations, and among the several states, and with the Indian tribes—for regulating *bankruptcies,* weights and measures, post-offices and post-roads, and captures on land and water—for establishing a uniform rule of naturalization, and for promoting the progress of science and useful arts—for defining and punishing piracies and felonies committed on the high seas, the offences of counterfeiting the securities and current coin of the United States, and offences against the law of nations, and for regulating all maritime concerns—for *organizing, arming and disciplining* the militia (the respective states training them, and appointing the officers)—for *calling them forth* when wanted, and for governing them when in the service of the union—for the *sole and exclusive government* of a federal city or town, not exceeding ten miles square, and of places ceded for forts, magazines, arsenals, dock-yards, and other needful buildings—for granting letters of marque and reprisal, and making war—for regulating the *times, places,* and *manner of holding elections* for senators and representatives—for making and concluding all treaties, and carrying them into execution—for judicially deciding all questions arising on the constitution, laws, and treaties of the union, in law and equity, and questions arising on state laws also, where ambassadors, other public ministers, and consuls, where the United States, individual states, or a state, where *citizens of different states,* and where foreign states, or a *foreign subject,* are parties or party—for impeaching and trying federal officers—for deciding on elections, and for expelling members, &c. All these enumerated powers we must examine and contemplate in all their extent and various branches, and then reflect, that the federal head will have full power to make all laws whatever respecting them;

and for carrying into full effect all powers vested in the union, in any
department, or officers of it, by the constitution, in order to see the full
extent of the federal powers, which will be supreme, and exercised by that
head at pleasure, conforming to the few limitations mentioned in the constitution. Indeed, I conceive, it is impossible to see them in their full extent at
present: we see vast undefined powers lodged in a weak organization, but
cannot, by the enquiries of months and years, clearly discern them in all their
numerous branches. These powers in feeble hands, must be tempting objects
for ambition and a love of power and fame.

But, say the advocates, they are all necessary for forming an energetic
federal government; all necessary in the hands of the union, for the common
defence and general welfare. In these great points they appear to me to go
from the end to the means, and from the means to the end, perpetually
begging the question. I think in the course of these letters, I shall sufficiently
prove, that some of these powers need not be lodged in the hands of the
union—that others ought to be exercised under better checks, and in part, by
the agency of the states—some I have already considered, some in my mind,
are not liable to objections, and the others, I shall briefly notice in this closing
letter.

The power to controul the military forces of the country, as well as the
revenues of it, requires serious attention. Here again, I must premise, that a
federal republic is a compound system, made up of constituent parts, each
essential to the whole: we must then expect the real friends of such a system
will always be very anxious for the security and preservation of each part, and
to this end, that each constitutionally possess its natural portion of power and
influence—and that it will constantly be an object of concern to them, to see
one part armed at all points by the constitution, and in a manner destructive
in the end, even of its own existence, and the others left constitutionally
defenceless.

The military forces of a free country may be considered under three
general descriptions—1. The militia. 2. the navy—and 3. the regular
troops—and the whole ought ever to be, and understood to be, in strict
subordination to the civil authority; and that regular troops, and select corps,
ought not to be kept up without evident necessity. Stipulations in the
constitution to this effect, are perhaps, too general to be of much service,
except merely to impress on the minds of the people and soldiery, that the
military ought ever to be subject to the civil authority, &c. But particular
attention, and many more definite stipulations, are highly necessary to render the military safe, and yet useful in a free government; and in a federal
republic, where the people meet in distinct assemblies, many stipulations are
necessary to keep a part from transgressing, which would be unnecessary
checks against the whole met in one legislature, in one entire government.—A militia, when properly formed, are in fact the people themselves, and render regular troops in a great measure unnecessary. The powers

to form and arm the militia, to appoint their officers, and to command their services, are very important; nor ought they in a confederated republic to be lodged, solely, in any one member of the government. First, the constitution ought to secure a genuine and guard against a select militia, by providing that the militia shall always be kept well organized, armed, and disciplined, and include, according to the past and general usage of the states, all men capable of bearing arms; and that all regulations tending to render this general militia useless and defenceless, by establishing select corps of militia, or distinct bodies of military men, not having permanent interests and attachments in the community to be avoided. I am persuaded, I need not multiply words to convince you of the value and solidity of this principle, as it respects general liberty, and the duration of a free and mild government: having this principle well fixed by the constitution, then the federal head may prescribe a general uniform plan, on which the respective states shall form and train the militia, appoint their officers and solely manage them, except when called into the service of the union, and when called into that service, they may be commanded and governed by the union. This arrangement combines energy and safety in it; it places the sword in the hands of the solid interest of the community, and not in the hands of men destitute of property, of principle, or of attachment to the society and government, who often form the select corps of peace or ordinary establishments: by it, the militia are the people, immediately under the management of the state governments, but on a uniform federal plan, and called into the service, command, and government of the union, when necessary for the common defence and general tranquility. But, say gentlemen, the general militia are for the most part employed at home in their private concerns, cannot well be called out, or be depended upon; that we must have a select militia; that is, as I understand it, particular corps or bodies of young men, and of men who have but little to do at home, particularly armed and disciplined in some measure, at the public expense, and always ready to take the field. These corps, not much unlike regular troops, will ever produce an inattention to the general militia; and the consequence has ever been, and always must be, that the substantial men, having families and property, will generally be without arms, without knowing the use of them, and defenceless; whereas, to preserve liberty, it is essential that the whole body of the people always possess arms, and be taught alike, especially when young, how to use them; nor does it follow from this, that all promiscuously must go into actual service on every occasion. The mind that aims at a select militia, must be influenced by a truly anti-republican principle; and when we see many men disposed to practice upon it, whenever they can prevail, no wonder true republicans are for carefully guarding against it. As a farther check, it may be proper to add, that the militia of any state shall not remain in the service of the union, beyond a given period, without the express consent of the state legislature.

As to the navy, I do not see that it can have any connection with the local

governments. The want of employment for it, and the want of monies in the
hands of the union, must be its proper limitation. The laws for building or
increasing it, as all the important laws mentioned in a former letter, touching
military and money matters, may be checked by requiring the attendance of a
large proportion of the representatives, and the consent of a large proportion
of those present, to pass them as before mentioned.

By art. 1. sect. 8. "Congress shall have *power to provide for* organizing,
arming, and disciplining the militia": *power to provide for*—does this imply any
more than power to prescribe a general uniform plan? And must not the
respective states pass laws (but in conformity to the plan) for forming and
training the militia.

In the present state of mankind, and of conducting war, the government of
every nation must have power to raise and keep up regular troops: the
question is, how shall this power be lodged? In an entire government, as in
Great-Britain, where the people assemble by their representatives in one
legislature, there is no difficulty, it is of course properly lodged in that
legislature: But in a confederated republic, where the organization consists of
a federal head, and local governments, there is no one part in which it can be
solely, and safely lodged. By art. 1. sect. 8. "congress shall have power to raise
and support armies," &c. By art. 1. sect. 10. "no state, without the consent of
congress, shall keep troops, or ships of war, in time of peace." It seems fit the
union should direct the raising of troops, and the union may do it in two ways;
by requisitions on the states, or by direct taxes—the first is most conformable
to the federal plan, and safest; and it may be improved, by giving the union
power, by its own laws and officers, to raise the state's quota that may neglect,
and to charge it with the expence; and by giving a fixed quorum of the state
legislatures power to disapprove the requisition. There would be less danger
in this power to raise troops, could the state governments keep a proper
controul over the purse and over the militia; but after all the precautions we
can take, without evidently fettering the union too much, we must give a
large accumulation of powers to it, in these and other respects. There is one
check, which, I think, may be added with great propriety—that is, no land
forces shall be kept up, but by legislative acts annually passed by congress,
and no appropriation of monies for their support shall be for a longer term
than one year. This is the constitutional practice in Great-Britain, and the
reasons for such checks in the United States appear to be much stronger. We
may also require that these acts be passed by a special majority, as before
mentioned. There is another mode still more guarded, and which seems to be
founded in the true spirit of a federal system: it seems proper to divide those
powers we can with safety, lodge them in no one member of the government
alone; yet substantially to preserve their use, and to ensure duration to the
government, by modifying the exercise of them—it is to empower congress
to raise troops by direct levies, not exceeding a given number, say 2000 in
time of peace, and 12,000 in a time of war, and for such further troops as may

be wanted, to raise them by requisitions qualified as before mentioned. By the above recited clause no state shall keep troops, &c. in time of peace—this clearly implies, it may do it in time of war: this must be on the principle, that the union cannot defend all parts of the republic, and suggests an idea very repugnant to the general tendency of the system proposed, which is to disarm the state governments: a state in a long war may collect forces sufficient to take the field against the neighbouring states. This clause was copied from the confederation, in which it was of more importance than in the plan proposed, because under this the separate states, probably, will have but small revenues.

By article 1. section 8. congress shall have power to establish uniform laws on the subject of bankruptcies, throughout the United States. It is to be observed, that the separate states have ever been in possession of the power, and in the use of it, of making bankrupt laws, militia laws, and laws in some other cases, respecting which, the new constitution, when adopted, will give the union power to legislate, &c.—but no words are used by the constitution to exclude the jurisdiction of the several states, and whether they will be excluded or not, or whether they and the union will have concurrent jurisdiction or not, must be determined by inference; and from the nature of the subject, if the power, for instance, to make uniform laws on the subject of bankruptcies, is in its nature, indivisible, or incapable of being exercised by two legislatures independently, or by one in aid of the other, then the states are excluded, and cannot legislate at all on the subject, even though the union should neglect or find it impracticable to establish uniform bankrupt laws. How far the union will find it practicable to do this, time only can fully determine. When we consider the extent of the country, and the very different ideas of the different parts in it, respecting credit, and the mode of making men's property liable for paying their debts, we may, I think, with some degree of certainty, conclude that the union never will be able to establish such laws; but if practicable, it does not appear to me, on further reflection, that the union ought to have the power; it does not appear to me to be a power properly incidental to a federal head, and, I believe, no one ever possessed it; it is a power that will immediately and extensively interfere with the internal police of the separate states, especially with their administering justice among their own citizens. By giving this power to the union, we greatly extend the jurisdiction of the federal judiciary, as all questions arising on bankrupt laws, being laws of the union, even between citizens of the same state, may be tried in the federal courts; and I think it may be shewn, that by the help of these laws, actions between citizens of different states, and the laws of the federal city, aided by no overstrained judicial fictions, almost all civil causes may be drawn into those courts. We must be sensible how cautious we ought to be in extending unnecessarily the jurisdiction of those courts, for reasons I need not repeat. This article of power too, will considerably increase, in the hands of the union, an accumulation of powers, some of a federal and some of a unfederal nature, too large without it.

The constitution provides, that congress shall have the sole and exclusive government of what is called the federal city, a place not exceeding ten miles square, and of all places ceded for forts, dock-yards, &c. I believe this is a novel kind of provision in a federal republic; it is repugnant to the spirit of such a government, and must be founded in an apprehension of a hostile disposition between the federal head and the state governments; and it is not improbable, that the sudden retreat of congress from Philadelphia, first gave rise to it.—With this apprehension, we provide, the government of the union shall have secluded places, cities, and castles of defence, which no state laws whatever shall invade. When we attentively examine this provision in all its consequences, it opens to view scenes almost without bounds. A federal, or rather a national city, ten miles square, containing a hundred square miles, is about four times as large as London; and for forts, magazines, arsenals, dock-yards, and other needful buildings, congress may possess a number of places or towns in each state. It is true, congress cannot have them unless the state legislatures cede them; but when once ceded, they never can be re- covered, and though the general temper of the legislatures may be averse to such cessions, yet many opportunities and advantages may be taken of particular times and circumstances of complying assemblies, and of particular parties, to obtain them. It is not improbable, that some considerable towns or places, in some intemperate moments, or influenced by anti-republican principles, will petition to be ceded for the purposes mentioned in the provision. There are men, and even towns, in the best republics, which are often fond of withdrawing from the government of them, whenever occasion shall present. The case is still stronger; if the provision in question holds out allurements to attempt to withdraw, the people of a state must ever be subject to state as well as federal taxes; but the federal city and places will be subject only to the latter, and to them by no fixed proportion; nor of the taxes raised in them, can the separate states demand any account of congress.— These doors opened for withdrawing from the state governments entirely, may, on other accounts, be very alluring and pleasing to those anti-republican men who prefer a place under the wings of courts.

If a federal town be necessary for the residence of congress and the public officers, it ought to be a small one, and the government of it fixed on republican and common law principles, carefully enumerated and established by the constitution. It is true, the states, when they shall cede places, may stipulate, that the laws and government of congress in them, shall always be formed on such principles; but it is easy to discern, that the stipulations of a state, or of the inhabitants of the place ceded, can be of but little avail against the power and gradual encroachments of the union. The principles ought to be established by the federal constitution, to which all the states are parties;

but in no event can there be any need of so large a city and places for forts, &c. totally exempted from the laws and jurisdictions of the state governments. If I understand the constitution, the laws of congress, constitutionally made, will have complete and supreme jurisdiction to all federal purposes, on every inch of ground in the United States, and exclusive jurisdiction on the high seas, and this by the highest authority, the consent of the people. Suppose ten acres at West-Point shall be used as a fort of the union, or a sea port town as a dock-yard, the laws of the union in those places respecting the navy, forces of the union, and all federal objects, must prevail, be noticed by all judges and officers, and executed accordingly: and I can discern no one reason for excluding from these places, the operation of state laws, as to mere state purposes; for instance, for the collection of state taxes in them, recovering debts, deciding questions of property arising within them on state laws, punishing, by state laws, theft, trespasses, and offences committed in them by mere citizens against the state laws.

The city and all the places in which the union shall have this exclusive jurisdiction, will be immediately under one entire government, that of the federal head; and be no part of any state, and consequently no part of the United States. The inhabitants of the federal city and places, will be as much exempt from the laws and controul of the state governments, as the people of Canada or Nova Scotia will be. Neither the laws of the states respecting taxes, the militia, crimes or property, will extend to them; nor is there a single stipulation in the constitution, that the inhabitants of this city, and these places, shall be governed by laws founded on principles of freedom. All questions, civil and criminal, arising on the laws of these places, which must be the laws of congress, must be decided in the federal courts; and also, all questions that may, by such judicial fictions as these courts may consider reasonable, be supposed to arise within this city, or any of these places, may be brought into these courts; and by a very common legal fiction, any personal contract may be supposed to have been made in any place. A contract made in Georgia may be supposed to have been made in the federal city, in Pennsylvania; the courts will admit the fiction, and not in these cases, make it a serious question, where it was in fact made. Every suit in which an inhabitant of a federal district may be a party, of course may be instituted in the federal courts—also, every suit in which it may be alledged, and not denied, that a party in it is an inhabitant of such a district—also, every suit to which a foreign state or subject, the union, a state, citizens of different states, in fact, or by reasonable legal fictions, may be a party or parties: And thus, by means of bankrupt laws, federal districts, &c. almost all judicial business, I apprehend, may be carried into the federal courts, without essentially departing from the usual course of judicial proceedings. The courts in Great-Britain have acquired their powers, and extended, very greatly, their jurisdictions by such fictions and suppositions as I have mentioned. The constitution, in these points, certainly involves in it principles, and almost hidden cases, which may unfold, and in time exhibit consequences we hardly think of. The power of naturalization, when viewed in connection with the judicial powers and cases, is, in my mind, of very doubtful extent. By the constitution itself, the citizens of each state will be naturalized citizens of every state, to the general purposes of instituting suits, claiming the benefits of the laws, &c. And in order to give the federal courts jurisdiction of an action, between citizens of the same state, in common acceptation, may not a court allow the plaintiff to say, he is a citizen of one state, and the defendant a citizen of another, without carrying legal fictions so far, by any means, as they have been carried by the courts of King's Bench and Exchequer, in order to bring causes within their cognizance—Further, the federal city and districts, will be totally distinct from any state, and a citizen of a state will not of course be a subject of any of them; and to avail himself of the privileges and immunities of them, must he not be naturalized by congress in them? and may not congress make any proportion of the citizens of the states naturalized subjects of the federal city and districts, and thereby entitle them to sue or defend, in all cases, in the federal courts? I have my doubts, and many sensible men, I find, have their doubts, on these points; and we ought to observe, they must be settled in the courts of law, by their rules, distinctions, and fictions. To avoid many of these intricacies and difficulties, and to avoid the undue and unnecessary extension of the federal judicial powers, it appears to me, that no federal districts ought to be allowed, and no federal city or town, except perhaps a small town, in which the government shall be republican, but in which congress shall have no jurisidiction over the inhabitants, but in common with the other inhabitants of the states. Can the union want, in such a town, any thing more than a right to the soil on which it may set its buildings, and extensive jurisdiction over the federal buildings, and property, its own members, officers, and servants in it? As to all federal objects, the union will have complete jurisdiction over them, of course anywhere, and everywhere. I still think that no actions ought to be allowed to be brought in the federal courts, between citizens of different states, at least, unless the cause be of very considerable importance; that no action against a state government, by any citizen or foreigner, ought to be allowed; and no action, in which a foreign subject is party, at least, unless it be of very considerable importance, ought to be instituted in the federal courts—I confess, I can see no reason whatever, for a foreigner, or for citizens of different states, carrying sixpenny causes into the federal courts; I think the state courts will be found by experience, to be bottomed on better principles, and to administer justice better than the federal courts.

The difficulties and dangers I have supposed, will result from so large a federal city, and federal districts, from the extension of the federal judicial powers, &c. are not, I conceive, merely possible, but probable. I think, pernicious political consequences will follow from them, and from the federal city especially, for very obvious reasons, a few of which I will mention.

We must observe, that the citizens of a state will be subject to state as well as federal taxes, and the inhabitants of the federal city and districts, only to such taxes as congress may lay—We are not to suppose all our people are attached to free government, and the principles of the common law, but that many thousands of them will prefer a city governed, not on republican principles—This city, and the government of it, must indubitably take their tone from the characters of the men, who from the nature of its situation and institution, must collect there. This city will not be established for productive labour, for mercantile, or mechanic industry; but for the residence of government, its officers and attendants. If hereafter it should ever become a place of trade and industry, in the early periods of its existence, when its laws and government must receive their fixed tone, it must be a mere court, with its appendages, the executive, congress, the law courts, gentlemen of fortune and pleasure, with all the officers, attendants, suitors, expectants and dependants on the whole, however brilliant and honourable this collection may be, if we expect it will have any sincere attachments to simple and frugal republicanism, to that liberty and mild government, which is dear to the laborious part of a free people, we most assuredly deceive ourselves. This early collection will draw to it men from all parts of the country, of a like political description: we see them looking towards the place already.

Such a city, or town, containing a hundred square miles, must soon be the great, the visible, and dazzling centre, the mistress of fashions, and the fountain of politics. There may be a free or shackled press in this city, and the streams which may issue from it may overflow the country, and they will be poisonous or pure, as the fountain may be corrupt or not. But not to dwell on a subject that must give pain to the virtuous friends of freedom, I will only add, can a free and enlightened people create a common head so extensive, so prone to corruption and salvery, as this city probably will be, when they have it in their power to form one pure and chaste, frugal and republican.

Under the confederation congress has no power whereby to govern its own officers and servant; a federal town, in which congress might have special jurisdiction, might be expedient; but under the new constitution, without a federal town, congress will have all necessary powers of course over its officers and servants; indeed it will have a complete system of powers to all the federal purposes mentioned in the constitution; so that the reason for a federal town under the confederation, will by no means exist under the constitution.—Even if a trial by jury should be admitted in the federal city, what man, with any state attachments or republican virtue about him, will submit to be tried by a jury of it.

I might observe more particularly upon several other parts of the constitution proposed; but it has been uniformly my object in examining a subject so extensive, and difficult in many parts to be illustrated, to avoid unimportant things, and not to dwell upon points not very material. The rule for apportioning requisitions on the states, having some time since been agreed to by eleven states, I have viewed as settled. The stipulation that congress, after twenty one years may prohibit the importation of slaves, is a point gained, if not so favourable as could be wished for. As monopolies in trade perhaps, can in no case be useful, it might not be amiss to provide expressly against them. I wish the power to reprieve and pardon was more cautiously lodged, and under some limitations. I do not see why congress should be allowed to consent that a person may accept a present, office, or title of a foreign prince, &c. As the state governments, as well as the federal are essential parts of the system, why should not the oath taken by the officers be expressly to support the whole? As to debts due to and from the union, I think the constitution intends, on examining art. 4. sect. 8. and art. 6 that they shall stand on the same ground under the constitution as under the confederation. In the article respecting amendments, it is stipulated that no state shall ever be deprived of its equal vote in the senate without its consent; and that alterations may be made by the consent of three-fourths of the states. Stipulations to bind the majority of the people may serve one purpose, to prevent frequent motions for change; but these attempts to bind the majority, generally give occasion for breach of contract. The states all agreed about seven years ago, that the confederation should remain unaltered, unless every state should agree to alterations: but we now see it agreed by the convention, and four states, that the old confederacy shall be destroyed, and a new one, of nine states, be erected, if nine only shall come in. Had we agreed, that a majority should alter the confederation, a majority's agreeing would have bound the rest: but now we must break the old league, unless all the states agree to alter, or not proceed with adopting the constitution. Whether the adoption by nine states will not produce a nearly equal and dangerous division of the people for and against the constitution—whether the circumstances of the country were such as to justify the hazarding a probability of such a situation, I shall not undertake to determine. I shall leave it to be determined hereafter, whether nine states, under a new federal compact, can claim the benefits of any treaties made with a confederation of thirteen, under a distinct compact and form of existence—whether the new confederacy can recover debts due to the old confederacy, or the arrears of taxes due from the states excluded.

It has been well observed, that our country is extensive, and has no external enemies to press the parts together: that, therefore, their union must depend on strong internal ties. I differ with the gentlemen who make these observations only in this, they hold the ties ought to be strengthened by a considerable degree of internal consolidation; and my object is to form them and strenghten them, on pure federal principles. Whatever may be the fate of many valuable and necessary amendments in the constitution proposed, the ample discussion and respectable opposition it will receive, will have a good effect—they will operate to produce a mild and prudent administration, and to put the wheels of the whole system in motion on proper principles—they will evince, that true republican principles and attachments are still alive and formidable in this country. These, in view, I believe, even men quite disposed to make a bad use of the system, will long hesitate before they will resolve to do it. A majority, from a view of our situation; and influenced by many considerations, may acquiese in the adoption of this constitution; but, it is evident that a very great majority of the people of the United States think it, in many parts, an unnecessary and unadviseable departure from true republican and federal principles.

The FEDERAL FARMER.

To the REPUBLICAN.

INDEX

LETTERS FROM THE FEDERAL FARMER

TO THE REPUBLICAN

was composed in VIP Garamond

by Bailey Typography, Inc., Nashville, Tennessee,

printed by Thomson-Shore, Inc., Dexter, Michigan,

and bound by John H. Dekker and Sons, Grand Rapids, Michigan.

Production: Paul R. Kennedy

Book and jacket design: Anna F. Jacobs